KU-167-357

ANIMAL ANTICS

BLITZ EDITIONS

Copyright © Bookmart Ltd 1994

All rights reserved. No part of this publication may be reproduced,
stored in a retrieval system, or transmitted in any form or by any
means, electronic, mechanical, photocopying, recording or otherwise,
without prior written permission from the publishers.

Published by Blitz Editions
an imprint of Bookmart Ltd
Registered Number 2372865
Trading as Bookmart Ltd, Desford Road, Enderby
Leicester LE9 5AD

This book was produced
by Amazon Publishing Ltd

Cover design: Peter Dolton
Text design: Jim Reader
Production Manager: Sue Gray
Editorial Manager: Roz Williams

Printed in the Slovak Republic

ISBN 1 85605 200 1

51733

This material has previously appeared in *Fame and Infamy*.

Every effort has been made to contact the copyright holders for the pictures.
In some cases they have been untraceable, for which we offer our apologies.
Thanks to the following picture libraries: Ancient Art & Architecture Collection (pp 55, 56, 57 top, 59 top, 66),
Associated Press courtesy of Hulton Deutsch (p 22), Brooke Bond Oxo Ltd (pp 20, 21),
Bruce Coleman Ltd (pp 39, 40 top, 41, 42 bottom, 43, 57 bottom, 59 bottom, 64),
Fortean Picture Library (pp 29, 30 left), Frank Spooner (pp 33 bottom, 67, 68),
Hulton Deutsch Collection Ltd (pp 2, 8, 9, 25, 36 bottom, 42 top, 44, 46, 51),
Popperfoto (pp 5 top, 14–16, 34, 37, 38, 65, 72), National Film Institute/Portfolio (p 23 top),
Rex Features (pp 11, 40 bottom, 45, 50, 71, 77), Jeff Spall (pp 33 top, 69),
Syndication International (pp 7, 10, 13, 17, 18 bottom, 19, 23 bottom, 35, 36 top, 47, 48, 49, 53, 60, 76),
Topham Picture Library (p 63).

Cover: The main picture and bottom left supplied by Hulton Deutsch Collection Ltd.
The bottom centre by Rex Features and the bottom right by Popperfoto.

The Authors
Karen Farrington is a journalist who has worked for both national newspapers, and as a freelance, for the best
selling weekly women's magazines. Her broad experience has brought her into contact with some of the most
intriguing mysteries, compelling crimes and moving animal stories of recent times.

Nick Constable, also a journalist, has spent many years working in Fleet Street and covered top stories including
the famine in Ethiopia, the government-backed assassinations of street children in Brazil and the Gulf War.
He has also worked extensively to expose cruelty to animals in Britain and around the world.

ANIMAL
ANTICS

TOUCHING TALES

The terrorists thought it would be child's play to steal the world's fastest racehorse, but their naive miscalculations were to result in the ignoble destruction of the magnificent stallion.

Streaking stallion Shergar galloped to glory in fine style, winning four major races in a year. He was perhaps the greatest flat racer ever to have lived.

But one dark night he vanished from his stable, never to be seen again. The shock disappearance made headlines across the globe. What can have happened to the fantastic thoroughbred with the famous white blaze? Soon the story ranked alongside the great mysteries of the age and was spoken of in the same breath as the ghost ship *Marie Celeste* and the runaway British nobleman Lord Lucan who disappeared the night his children's nanny was murdered.

There were periodic sightings of Shergar alive and well and living in Libya, the Channel Islands and the Isle of Man. As late as 1992, bounty hunters tried to claim thousands of pounds from an insurance company on the basis that the horse lived and bred, ignoring the difficulties there would be in registering the birth of any offspring. Observers speculated about a Mafia plot or an arch-criminal taking vengeful action against the horse's wealthy owner, the Aga Khan.

But sadly it seems Shergar probably died only hours after he went missing. It seems the horse was the target of the IRA, terrorists from Northern Ireland. Detectives hired soon afterwards came to the conclusion it was a terrorist kidnap gang responsible for the snatch and that it was probably bungled.

HORSE THIEVES

In 1992 their theories were confirmed when IRA informer Sean O'Callaghan spoke out about the crime from his prison cell in Maghaberry, Belfast.

Opposite: *Shergar won the 1981 Derby in classic style. His performance was the stuff of* **Boys' Own** *fiction – 19-year-old jockey Walter Swinburn had never dared dream he would romp home ten lengths clear.*

Below: *The stable from which Shergar was snatched by IRA terrorists.*

WITH FLARING NOSTRILS
THE HIGHLY STRUNG
STALLION SCENTED DANGER
– HE REARED UP TO STRIKE
AT HIS ABDUCTORS WITH
DEADLY HOOVES.

He told how on the night of 8 February 1983 a masked gang crept stealthily onto the rural Irish stud farm which was home to Shergar. It was the start of their ambitious cash-raising escapade and everything was set for an international coup.

Shergar had by this time retired from racing. His days of sprinting splendour were over now he had notched up £436,000 worth of prize money. His victory in the 1981 Epsom Derby by 10 lengths with 19-year-old Walter Swinburn in the saddle was but a memory. His winning form in the Irish Derby and the King George VI & Queen Elizabeth Diamond Stakes at Ascot in the same year had faded from the minds of all but the most ardent racegoers.

But Shergar still had his most productive cash-spinning days ahead of him. He was going to stud, visiting 50 mares a year and commanding fees of about £75,000 a time. His owner, the Aga Khan, had sold 34 shares in the wonder horse to prominent society people including Robert Sangster, Lord Derby, Stavros Niarchos and Sheikh Maktoum Al Maktoum. From silky muzzle to flicking tail, Shergar was worth £10 million. There would be a lot of influential people anxious for the safe return of Shergar once he was gone and the IRA knew it.

So under the leadership of racing fan Kevin Mallon, a fervent IRA activist recently released from a jail term for attempted murder, the gang of up to nine men moved in.

Astonishingly, there were no effective security measures for them to breach at the stud in Ballymany, County Kildare, within sight of the famous Curragh racecourse. The token measure to guard against intruders, a surveillance camera system, was faulty. It left the horse thieves ample opportunity to tow in the horsebox in which they were going to spirit away their prize.

Communicating by walkie-talkie, the gang thought the operation was a cinch – until it came to handling Shergar. While everything else may have been meticulously planned, Mallon and his cronies blundered because they had no idea how highly strung a stallion of Shergar's calibre could be. The horse could sense danger and maybe even impending doom. With flared nostrils, he reared up time and time again with an angry neigh. Here was quite a different animal from the docile creature the abductors were anticipating. By the time they were 100 miles north of the farm Shergar was in a frenzy and was injuring himself in his torment. There was no option but to shoot the poor, crazed beast.

O'Callaghan told how the body of Shergar was hurriedly buried in the Ballinamore region of County Leitrim, never again to be found amid the rocky landscape.

Meanwhile, police on both sides of the Irish border mounted a huge search. It was the biggest police hunt Eire had known. Top detectives even consulted 50 clairvoyants and psychics in the hope of recovering the horse.

Although a £2 million ransom demand was duly delivered by the kidnappers, the Aga Khan refused to pay.

It was the beginning of a string of kidnaps by the IRA, including an attempt to capture Galen Weston, the Canadian supermarket tycoon. Fooled into thinking Weston was a sitting duck at his rambling home in County Wicklow in August 1983, the gang struck again, but in fact the wealthy target was in England playing polo with the Prince of Wales. Instead, there was a band of armed police who managed to hold most of the six-member gang despite a shootout.

So now most of the kidnappers of Shergar were put behind bars although they were never brought to justice for killing the classic animal. The policeman in charge of the case, Superintendent Jim Murphy, has disclosed he knows the identities of the killers but never found enough evidence to bring them to trial.

In their wake they left an unsavoury insurance wrangle which still rumbles on today. Many of the shareholders recovered their stakes through cover-all insurance policies, but some companies refused to pay out until they received proof that Shergar was finally dead. Even the revelations by O'Callaghan failed to persuade them the horse had been killed. The fact the horse was stolen wasn't enough to secure payout. One man, Dublin vet Stan Cosgrove, lost his house and ran into huge debt after borrowing heavily with his brother to buy a share in Shergar.

Now a six-year time limit for claims appears to exclude the unlucky few left out of pocket to the tune of £250,000 by the sad affair.

IRA BRUTALITY

Army horse Sefton was also the victim of brutal cruelty on his home turf at the hands of heartless IRA bombers.

It should have been a proud and prestigious occasion for Sefton and his troop in Hyde Park on that fateful day in 1982. Horses and men were kitted out in their finery for ceremonial duties. Little did they realize they were to be cut down by a car bomb packed with nails planted by the IRA.

Four men and seven horses died. Sefton was as close to death as a horse could get, with savage injuries inflicted after he took the full force of the blast. He suffered 38 wounds including a deep cut to his jugular vein. It seemed his life would ebb away. But one man was determined to save him: Army vet Major Noel Carding spent an hour and a half treating the bloodied gashes and, amid the scene of carnage, saved his life.

The photograph of the injuries to Sefton's face and body flashed around the world and said more about the terrible consequences of the bomb blast than a million words. Convalescing in his stable, he received hundreds of get-well gifts and cards.

Within months, Sefton proved to the world he was a fighter. He made a feted first public appearance after the blast: at the

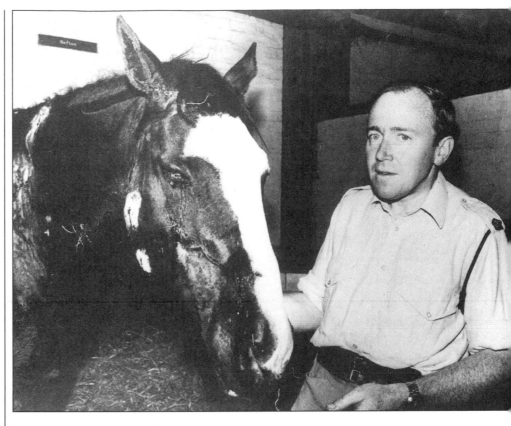

Above: *Sefton with the Army vet who saved his life, Major Noel Carding. The horse suffered 38 separate wounds from flying nails.*

Left: *Sefton didn't take easily to the pomp and ceremony of life in the Household Cavalry.*

Above: *Sefton with Trooper Pederson. In his own way, Sefton hit back at the terrorists responsible for maiming him. He raised thousands of pounds for forces' charities.*

THE CRUEL 6-INCH NAILS CUT THE VELVETY FLESH OF THE HORSES TO RIBBONS.

---

prestige Horse of the Year Show in London, side by side with Echo, the police horse also hurt in the explosion.

Questions were asked in the House of Commons as to whether both horses should be awarded medals of honour.

With pride, the horse the IRA couldn't kill took his place back in the ranks and reassumed the royal role for which he had been trained. He worked for another two years before retiring in 1984 with 15 years' service to his credit.

Sefton had been born in Ireland in 1963 and was 3 years old when he caught the eye of a purchasing officer from the British Army charged with buying at least 50 horses a year for the cavalry. But there was no hint of the glory to come when, known simply as 5816, he was hustled onto a ferry, one of 37 horses making the arduous journey from Ireland to new pastures in England.

Sefton was ebony in colour but for his four white socks and substantial blaze – which indicated early on he was a horse with character. It is well known among horse handlers that the animals bearing white marks are the liveliest of the bunch.

This gelding also had a wicked eye that glinted with mischief and, true to the old saying, he was not the easiest horse to manage. But his abundant spirit appealed to the Army's horse experts. He was picked for duty with the Royal Horse Guards and christened Sefton after an earl from the same regiment who had served with distinction in two world wars and later became Lord Mayor of Liverpool.

It takes months to train a horse to remain calm in the face of brass bands, traffic, and rowdy people, not to mention wearing cumbersome regalia. By 1968 Sefton was put on trial to see if he was ready to go on parade. He failed the test.

Nevertheless, he was brought out looking splendid for the 1968 Trooping of the Colour before the queen. Hating every minute of the pomp and pageantry, he skittered and reared, distinguishing himself only as the worst behaved horse of the day.

It wasn't until three months later that he passed the Horse Guards' test of excellence and moved on to daily duties around some of the most majestic landmarks of London. He became a familiar sight around Whitehall, the Victoria Monument and Pall Mall.

Afterwards, he had a spell at a training school and in Germany with the North Atlantic Treaty Organization forces before returning to Wellington Barracks, central London.

He took part in the Queen's Silver Jubilee celebrations and the Royal Wedding street procession following the vows sworn at St Paul's Cathedral by Prince Charles and Lady Diana Spencer. Gradually Sefton put his skittish days behind him, becoming a veteran of the Royal Parade and even winning prizes for his demeanour.

It seemed a day just like any other when Sefton and the rest of the troop set off on 20 July 1982 from the barrack stables to the Whitehall sentry posts. But at 10.40 am a huge explosion ripped the parading pack to pieces. Using remote control, the terrorists detonated a 25 lb gelignite bomb stuffed with 30 lb of 6 in and 4 in nails which cut the velvet flesh of the horses to ribbons. Sefton had a nail in his head, a scorched eyeball, metal remains of the car in his neck, and was gushing with blood from his wounds.

Given only a fifty-fifty chance of survival, he had none the less fared better than stablemates Yeastvite, Epaulette, Rochester, Waterford, Falcon, Zara and Cedric, all of whom perished.

The wounds would take months to heal. But Sefton's indomitable spirit had captured the hearts and minds of the world. He became a symbol of survival and endurance in the face of cowardice and horror. As the outrage was followed the same day by another bomb which killed seven bandsmen in Regent's Park, feelings were running high. Each member of the royal family sent messages of sympathy to the barracks. The public rallied by donating £100,000, fruit, vegetables and some 250,000 Polo mints. Sefton became a celebrity, helping to raise thousands of pounds for forces' charitable funds.

It was an emotional moment when he finally left the Hyde Park barracks for the last time. The Band of the Blues and Royals played 'Auld Lang Syne' and the 'Black Horse' as his horsebox was marched regally out of the front gates.

His destination was the Home of Rest for Horses at Speen Farm near Princes Risborough, Buckinghamshire, where he happily accepted the adulation of visitors, especially when they showed their appreciation with a sugar lump or biscuit.

The end came for Sefton only when he became lame at the age of 30 years. Despite the efforts of vets at the Defence Animal Centre's Veterinary Hospital in Melton Mowbray, Leicestershire, he was put down in July 1993.

AGAINST THE ODDS

Everyone loves a winner and Red Rum was revered more than most victorious horses. The very name Red Rum became a byword for success in Britain as the tremendous horse stormed past the post ahead of the field three times in the country's toughest race, the Grand National.

But the affection and esteem Rummy commanded wasn't just for his astonishing abilities over the jumps and in the field. Here was a horse who made it to the top of

Above: *Sefton and his rider, Trooper Michael Pederson, launch the horse's biography. With them are* (**from left**) *celebrities Brough Scott, Anita Harris and Barbara Woodhouse.*

Above: *Red Rum on one of his regular beach gallops.*

Below: *Red Rum wins his third Grand National, in 1977.*

his profession against all the odds: he was a back-street kid who made it to the big time. When jockeys and trainers were blind to his talents and ran him ragged, he was determined to win through. He even beat a crippling illness before clinching the title of Britain's best-loved horse.

He was bred for flat racing, not the hurdles where he made his name. It didn't augur well when his mother was declared mad. With this dubious heritage, Rummy was bought and sold three times in quick succession. Even now, he was determined to distinguish himself. Aged just 2, he won his first race. His prize for the triumph over five furlongs was a mere £133.

But his existence was loveless and bleak until a chance meeting in a taxi cab put him on the road to stardom.

The taxi fare was Noel le Mare, the son of a missionary who started a civil engineering business with just a few pounds in his pocket. Years later his company, Norwest Holst, was a multi-million pound enterprise. But Le Mare, now in his 80s, wasn't satisfied.

Back in 1906 he had witnessed Grand National mania on the streets of Liverpool after Ascetic's Silver roared to victory. It was his dream to own a Grand National winner of his own.

The cabbie was struggling horse-trainer Ginger McCain. Down on his luck, McCain was forced behind the wheel to

earn cash when three seasons as a trainer bought him only three winners. But he had enough energy and enthusiasm to impress Le Mare, who charged him to find the Grand National winner he yearned for.

In August 1972 McCain found Rummy at Doncaster Sales and paid 6,000 guineas of Le Mare's cash for him. The horse was 7 years old and had already been through five trainers. He was also suffering pedalostitis, a crumbling of the foot's main bone that was usually incurable. But at last here was someone who would cherish him and have the faith needed to bring out the best bubbling underneath in Rummy.

McCain nearly gave up when he realized the animal on which his hopes were pinned was lame, but regular gallops in the sand and sea at Southport were to provide an unexpected and enduring cure. His stable was as humble as his training ground: it was a tumbledown shack behind McCain's second-hand-car showroom. But nothing was going to hold this horse back. Excitement mounted when Red Rum won race after race. With five victories behind him, he lined up for the first time at the start of the 1973 Grand National. As usual, the course was buzzing with excitement and throbbing with anticipation. It was an

atmosphere Red Rum relished. It was a pounding, grinding race with a nail-biting finish. Crisp was ahead and looked certain to win the coveted trophy, but Red Rum had other ideas and produced astonishing

Above: *A farewell to Aintree. Red Rum makes his last appearance on the course that made his name.*

THE STRUGGLING HORSE-TRAINER SENSED THE SPIRIT IN THE CRIPPLED NAG.

Left: *In retirement Rummy was as busy as ever. Here he opens a betting shop in north London.*

speed and drive which left spectators gasping. He overtook Crisp, won the race and knocked 19 seconds off the course record. He returned in 1974 to repeat his victory, by now the nation's favourite race horse. Red Rum revelled in the gruelling course, labelled cruel by animal rights' demonstrators. The following two years saw him pipped at the post but he wasn't satisfied at the thought of bowing out as second best: he would go for the hat-trick.

In 1977 McCain was once again to be found at the centre of the hubbub at Aintree on Grand National Day. 'Everybody, it seemed, wanted me to win the National a third time. The horse had so much presence that year,' he recalled. 'He virtually owned Aintree. It was uncanny.'

Red Rum didn't let his fans down. He romped home with 25 lengths to spare. Only a foot injury stopped him competing in 1978, an old man of 13 years of age.

The fracture which put an end to his Grand National days put him out of racing for ever, but he had notched up an incredible record. He had won a quarter of all the races around the jumps he had entered. His prize money totalled a record £115,000.

When owner Le Mare died, the horse passed to Ginger McCain, the man who had made him great. Still oozing with personality and popularity, Red Rum found himself at the centre of fresh thrills. He was invited to open supermarkets and fetes and appear at bashes alongside other celebrities. Soon he was the first horse in Britain to become a company. Red Rum Ltd was even more profitable than Red Rum, the racer. Within a few years, his appearance fees had soared into the £200,000 bracket. A decade later and the amount was more than £1 million.

But Red Rum was held in special regard

Below: *A terrified Misty is hauled through the streets during a Spanish fiesta in 1990.*

by the British people. He was a back-street kid who made good through guts, dedication and sheer hard work. In 1991 it seemed the end of the track had finally come for Red Rum when a sudden illness threatened his life. Against all odds, Rummy fought back and once again was the winner, returning to good health, to the relief of his owner and horse lovers across the country.

BEASTS OF BURDEN

The front pages of Britain's newspapers are usually the reserve of politicians and stars involved in outrage or scandal. It's rare that any animal makes it big in the media, let alone a humble donkey.

But that's just what Blackie, the ill-fated donkey from Spain, did back in 1987.

His mournful eyes gazed from every newspaper as his woeful plight was exposed. He grabbed the headlines with an extraordinary story which would make him the most famous donkey in the world.

His tale started in the sun-baked mountain village of Villanueva de la Vera. It is only 140 miles from the cosmopolitan Spanish capital of Madrid but it might as well be in a different country.

For the village still observes ancient fiestas involving appalling cruelty to animals which leave the rest of the world wincing. Despite growing unease in Spain – where 83 per cent of the population opposes blatant torture of animals – the locals involved were prepared to risk their public image for the sake of some dubious fiesta frolics.

Blackie would spend 364 days of every year unnoticed and unloved in a field. But

Above: *Peace at last. After the horrors of fiesta time Blackie lived out his last years in the care of the Sidmouth donkey sanctuary, southern England.*

on Shrove Tuesday came his moment of gory glory. On that day the villagers mark the capture of an evil rapist hundreds of years ago with the Fiesta del Pero-Palo.

Traditionally, the chosen donkey is locked in the village hall with young men fired up by drink and the relentless pursuit of 'pleasure' is on. The donkey is forced to join the revelry as bottles of spirit are poured down its throat. Then comes the street parade.

The heaviest man in the village is chosen to ride the donkey, whose legs are already buckling through the effects of drink. Behind them follows a chanting, jeering mass ready to push and shove the unfortunate animal if it falters.

Shaking and scarred across his rump, Blackie survived the ordeal at least once before one horrified animal lover and a host of British newspapers intervened.

Victoria Moore, half of a cabaret act with her guitar-playing husband, read about the impending fiesta and discovered there was little she could do from her home in Southport, Lancashire, to stop the atrocity. She announced her intention to visit the village personally to see what she could achieve.

Ignoring the death threat bearing a Spanish postmark which landed on her doormat, she set off for Spain, encountering a team of determined journalists en route. She describes her first stroll through the village as like something from the film *High Noon*. 'Residents stared at me from doorways and threw bangers,' she recalls.

By this time international journalists had joined their British counterparts, complete with TV camera crews, to observe the stand-off between the locals and the animal rights campaigner. Astonished at being the focus of such widespread attention, the Spaniards allowed Blackie to trot unfettered through the town before he was sold for £280. Mrs Moore was helped by one newspaper, the *Daily Star*, in returning Blackie to Britain, where he lived out his days at the country's largest donkey sanctuary, at Sidmouth, south Devon.

Journalists from the *Daily Star* were cock-a-hoop at securing the by-now famous donkey for themselves, thus getting the edge over their bitter Fleet Street rivals, *The Sun*. Yet *The Sun* was also claiming to have the redeemed donkey in its care. The

public at home were mystified. How could both sides be claiming victory when clearly only one donkey was at stake?

It seems a business-minded local man was at the heart of the confusion. He passed off a donkey to *The Sun* for a healthy number of pesetas, pretending it was Blackie. When *Star* journalists appeared, he claimed the donkey he had sold was actually a ringer for Blackie. Yet he was prepared to sell the real Blackie to the *Star* – for a price. That was how the *Star* journalists were able to return triumphant, leaving their opponents with some difficult explanations to make. There was talk of kidnap attempts on the rescued animal by the competitive hacks who had much more to lose than just readers. At the end of the affair one journalist did change jobs, switching from *The Sun* to the *Star*.

For six years Blackie retained his top status. Visitors poured through the gates of the sanctuary to meet the wiry haired donkey with a soft white muzzle who so narrowly escaped death and degradation at the hands of tormentors in search of fun.

He died aged around 20 in the sanctuary in May 1993 after a 10-day illness in which he stopped eating. Before being put down he was given a nibble of his favourite treat, a ginger biscuit, and then quietly died, leaving his girlfriend and paddock companion Lola desolate. He was buried in a marked grave within the boundaries of the sanctuary where he had finally found peace.

Sanctuary owner Dr Elizabeth Svendsen said: 'He was very weak and had come to the end of the road. We are heartbroken. But bearing in mind his very tough life and the trauma of the fiesta in Villanueva de la Vera, he has done very well to enjoy six years of happy, well-cared-for life in the sanctuary with Lola.'

Blackie fared better than Misty, his successor. His owner was the village mayor Felix Perez. But Senor Perez signed him over to a life of barbarism when he donated the 6-year-old to the village for use in the annual fiesta. Misty survived at least three fiestas despite the best attempts of the villagers to crush him under their combined weights.

Journalist Ed Owen witnessed the fiesta in 1990. 'A crowd of drunken revellers

THE APPALLING CRUELTY BEGAN AS BOTTLES OF SPIRITS WERE FORCIBLY POURED DOWN THE DONKEY'S THROAT.

surrounded the terrified donkey and careered uncontrollably around the village.

'I waded into the staggering mass of drunken humanity and found the donkey squashed on the cobbles, covered in sweat. Misty tried to raise his head as the heaving crowd endeavoured to lift him and remount. He was quivering as though having an epileptic fit, nostrils flared and shaking, foam dripping from his mouth.

'The poor animal was ruthlessly prodded and tugged as the raging yobs in Villanueva de la Vera forced him to rise on trembling legs.'

Misty's ordeal lasted 90 minutes, after which he had lost an estimated 50 lb in weight and his heart rate was double the norm.

Earlier in the 1980s the nightmare was too much for one of the donkeys, who died under the strain. His body was left floating in the village fountain.

Mrs Moore went on to found the charity FACE, Fight Animal Cruelty in Europe. She continues to battle for the halt of other fiestas which have sprung up around Spain following the demise of dictator Franco, who had banned them. Her efforts helped to stop the fiesta at Manganese de la Polvorosa in which live goats are thrown from the church tower. 'But the overall picture is bleak. Twenty-seven thousand bulls, cows and calves plus an unknown number of goats and chickens are tortured, raped, mutilated and killed very year in these events. There is a lot more to do.'

> **THE BEAST WAS SHAKING WITH TERROR AND FOAM WAS DRIPPING FROM HIS MOUTH.**

Below: *British animal lovers give Misty a health check before his ordeal.*

ANIMALS ON TV

Many animal stars of the screen will willingly 'die' for their art – again and again and again. Most are blissfully content with their roles and the endless titbits, but for an unfortunate few the demands made upon them can lead to tragedy.

Above: *Talk about hamming it up! Pippin shows it's snow joke when you're a star.*

Opposite: *Do I look cute or what? Pippin's appealing expressions won the hearts of millions.*

Show a director an actor who is keen to please, obedient and never throws a tantrum – and he will show you a star.

That's why the animals who are so familiar on our TV screens today are favoured by studio bosses. Professional from the tips of their damp noses to the end of their quivering tails, animals who appear on the box or in the cinema are trained to the peak of perfection.

Never work with children or animals, the old saying goes. However, while tots might give you a hard time, the schooled pet never will – as plenty of Hollywood directors would testify.

One of them, Joe Camp, was haunted by the moving story of a boy and his dog and the adventures they had together, mainly because they reminded him so much of his own happy childhood.

He managed to secure a small budget, then set about finding the stars. He had the pick of budding actors keen to cut their teeth on the happy home-on-the-range kind of story he was backing. But the pup star – the key to the success of the film, as Camp well knew – was a harder nut to crack.

CUTE CANINES

He scoured the kennels of Hollywood and the surrounding area looking for the perfect canine. Bloodhounds were too big, terriers too small and poodles all wrong.

One day Camp arrived at the Hollywood dog home run by Frank Inn and spotted the dog of his dreams. He found Higgins, an amiable mongrel, and knew instantly that his search was over.

Trouble was, Higgins was a veteran of the animal acting business and the star of a long-running and highly successful US TV series called *Petticoat Junction* along with Eddie Albert. He was also the grand old age of 11, mature by any standard in the dog world and about to be pensioned off for retirement.

Camp was determined his search would not be in vain. Together with owner Frank Inn he decided Higgins could make a glorious comeback, this time with the name Benji. It simply meant that a young relative by the name of Hazel was brought in to do some of the more energetic stunts.

The result was an overnight sensation. Everybody wanted to see *Benji*, released in 1974, which had the hero hound saving two children from kidnappers and earning a place in their grateful parents' home. It grossed $52 million in the days when

MOST ANIMAL STARS ADORE THE LIFE THEY LEAD — THEY BASK IN THE LIMELIGHT AND LOVE THE LIFE-STYLE.

blockbusters were rare if not unheard of. There were sequels in which Higgins was replaced by Benji II, a female this time but every inch as endearing as the original. The last Benji film to be made, in 1987, was *Benji the Hunted* and featured Benji III. This time the cute canine was living rough in the wild and saving threatened animals along the way.

Higgins, the grand old man of canine stars, founded an acting dynasty which went successfully transatlantic in the shape of his granddaughter, Pippin, now perhaps the best-known pooch in the business.

Pippin was given to Englishwoman Ann Head as a puppy just before she returned to Britain after a 7-year spell spent working in the USA. Ann worked alongside Frank Inn and was on the way to becoming one of the world's best-known animal trainers.

Everywhere she went, Pippin would shadow her, watching and learning as other animal stars went through their paces. And Pippin was hungry to learn.

As Ann points out, the only way a dog can be trained is to ensure it is blissfully happy.

'About 80 per cent of their ability comes from the environment they are in and 20 per cent is hereditary. My animals absolutely adore the life they lead. The secret is that they are incredibly contented and they aren't put under any pressure.'

Her animals must be not only good natured and patient, but also adaptable. They must be able to repeat a stunt a dozen or more times until the scene is perfect. Alternatively, rehearsed routines could be changed at any minute by a director seeing new angles so you must be able to teach an old dog new tricks at the drop of a hat. It takes years to tutor a dog until it reaches its peak.

'Unfortunately, 99.9 per cent of pets simply cannot cut the mustard, no matter how talented their owners believe them to be,' explains Ann, of Crowthorne, Berkshire.

Pippin is so gifted she even trotted off with two advertising industry Oscars in 1989 in Cannes, beating a 3,642-strong field of commercials from all over the world. The coveted Grand Prix awards are just a few of the honours she has achieved.

And she's no stranger to viewers of TV advertisements in Britain and Europe, while viewers as far flung as Japan and Taiwan have met Pippin through their TV screens.

Her range of skills has caused its fair share of problems for unsuspecting passers-by, however. Pippin is top dog when it comes to playing dead, and it was for this reason that she was picked to star in a police film narrated by actor Richard Briers about the dangers of telephone box vandalism. Liberal amounts of fake blood were applied and she draped herself over the arms of an actor who looked suitably sorrowful. But a passing motorist who obviously didn't see the camera poised on the other side of the road screeched to a halt and insisted on taking the apparently injured dog and devoted master to the vet's

The kind words dried up in the driver's mouth when the blood-splattered dog miraculously revived, jumped to the floor and began wagging her tail furiously.

Now aged 11 years, Pippin has her own stunt man, grandson Higgins, aged 2 and named after his famous great-great grandfather. In Pippin's latest starring role alongside actress Lynda Baron in children's TV series, Higgins was used for some of the physically demanding sequences.

Below: *Superdog Pippin was the animal star of the advertising industry. He even got two Oscars for his performances.*

A VERY IMPORTANT PUSS

Ann Head is also in charge of today's Arthur, successor to the king of cat stars. Arthur was the cat who came to fame thanks to a knockout left hook. It was his ability to scoop cat food out of a tin with a paw that brought the rather superior white feline to prominence.

The first Arthur made his TV debut in 1966. He may have been all white but he led a most colourful life. There was even confusion over whether he was really a she by the name of Samantha. Arthur became the talk of the country after being the subject of a court case and, later, a kidnap.

Arthur was apparently a stray found roaming in Hemel Hempstead in 1964 by actor Toneye Manning and was eventually adopted by Manning's friend, actress June Clyne.

Miss Clyne was astonished when she found the cat could help himself to food once the tin was opened. It was a simply a matter of preference. Nobody appeared to have taught him, yet he chose the paw. He was, she realized, an advertising man's dream but she refused to part with her beloved pet. Instead, she was willing to give cat food manufacturers Spillers a lifetime option which would have allowed Arthur star status while remaining at home. Sadly, Miss Clyne died before negotiations were completed.

Spillers went on to acquire Arthur for a highly successful advertising campaign when he put his foot in it time and time again and soon became a Very Important Puss. With rightful ownership unclear following the untimely death of Miss Clyne, Spillers paid her mother £600 and Toneye Manning £700 to secure all rights to the cat.

But Mr Manning was unhappy and took the case to court. He had not only found Arthur but had also married Miss Clyne, he insisted, the wedding having taken place aboard a ferry in the Irish Sea.

A mighty cat fight took place with both sides laying claim to Arthur. Each won victories in the first rounds of the battle with consecutive court rulings awarding Arthur first to Mr Manning, then to Spillers.

Mr Manning told how he delivered the prized puss to the Russian Embassy for asylum. When he refused to hand Arthur

over to Spillers he was jailed for contempt of court, serving 15 days in Brixton prison.

In court, he alleged Spillers was cruel to Arthur and even extracted his teeth to ensure he would eat out of the can.

The claim was emphatically denied by Spillers, who said that although Arthur was being treated for a gum disease no extractions had taken place.

Hearing the amazing case, Mr Justice Bridge turned dentist for a few moments when Arthur paraded along the bench and bared his teeth. Later the judge dismissed the cruelty allegations and in November 1969 decided the cat belonged to Spillers fair and square.

Arthur went to a cats' home in Essex to continue his career, pampered with a diet of fresh fish, steak, chicken and rabbit and at work only nine days a year. All was well for five years and then the mog found himself splashed over the front pages again after being snatched from his comfortable cattery home. By now Arthur was 14 years old – 98 in human terms – and there were genuine fears about his health.

No one knows what went on in those

Above: *This canny trick became Arthur the cat's trademark. He went on to star in £4 million-worth of TV commercials.*

IT WAS ALLEGED THAT THE PETFOOD COMPANY WAS CRUEL TO ARTHUR AND EVEN YANKED OUT HIS TEETH TO FORCE HIM TO EAT FROM THE CAN.

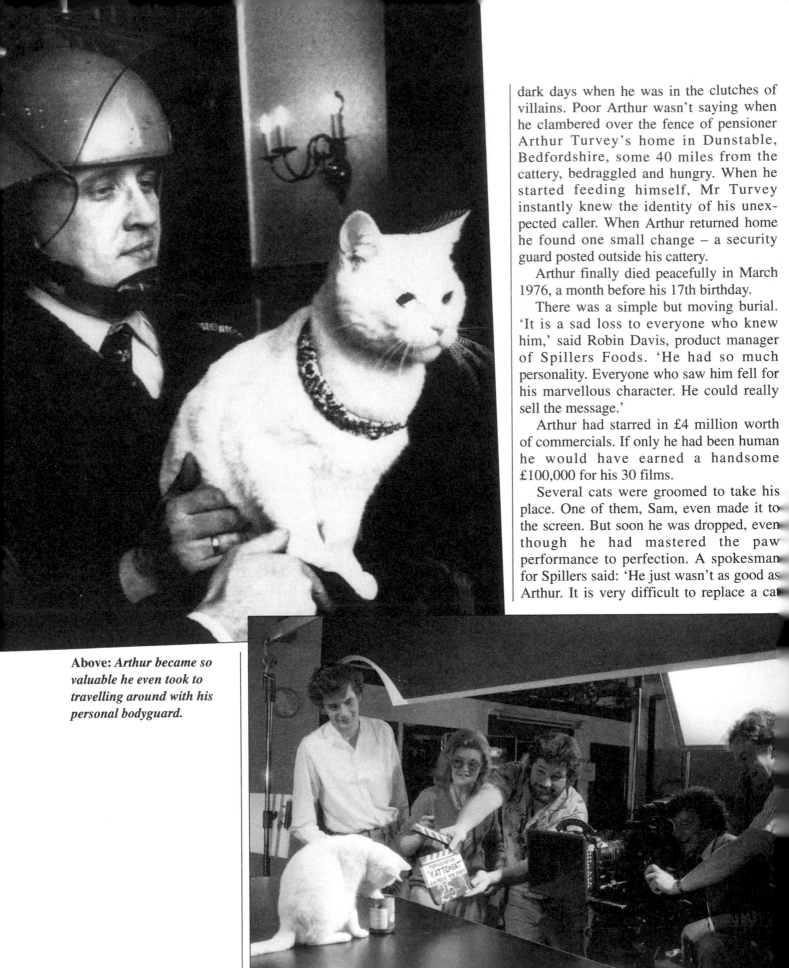

dark days when he was in the clutches of villains. Poor Arthur wasn't saying when he clambered over the fence of pensioner Arthur Turvey's home in Dunstable, Bedfordshire, some 40 miles from the cattery, bedraggled and hungry. When he started feeding himself, Mr Turvey instantly knew the identity of his unexpected caller. When Arthur returned home he found one small change – a security guard posted outside his cattery.

Arthur finally died peacefully in March 1976, a month before his 17th birthday.

There was a simple but moving burial. 'It is a sad loss to everyone who knew him,' said Robin Davis, product manager of Spillers Foods. 'He had so much personality. Everyone who saw him fell for his marvellous character. He could really sell the message.'

Arthur had starred in £4 million worth of commercials. If only he had been human he would have earned a handsome £100,000 for his 30 films.

Several cats were groomed to take his place. One of them, Sam, even made it to the screen. But soon he was dropped, even though he had mastered the paw performance to perfection. A spokesman for Spillers said: 'He just wasn't as good as Arthur. It is very difficult to replace a cat

Above: *Arthur became so valuable he even took to travelling around with his personal bodyguard.*

Right: *Lights. Action! The new Arthur settles into his role.*

THE NEW STAR WAS DISCOVERED CLOSE TO DEATH AND IN A TERRIBLE STATE, CALLOUSLY ABANDONED BY HIS FORMER OWNERS.

Left: *Legendary trainer Ann Head scoured the country in search of a successor to Arthur. She at last found Arthur II in a Hertfordshire, England, animal shelter. He was so ill after being abandoned that she had to talk a vet out of putting him down.*

like that. Now we are using big cats – lions – in our advertisements.'

But a decade later Spillers thought again about the success they had known with Arthur. The search was on for a replacement for King Arthur. Ann Head was the woman charged with the job of talent scout. Little did she realize the animal she sought was close to death, languishing in the Wood Green Animal Shelter in Royston, Hertfordshire.

He had been abandoned by a family which was moving and didn't want him any more.

Ann recalls: 'I picked him up and played with him for a few minutes. He looked ghastly and had lost interest in himself but I knew he was the right cat.'

He was so poorly she even had to talk a vet out of putting him to sleep. And sure enough, with lashings of tender love and care the new Arthur made a complete recovery.

'We have built up a good relationship, he will walk into any studio with a full crew and lights and just perform because he loves it,' says Ann.

Not only that, he makes regular celebrity appearances at cat shows around the country where he will offer his regal paw to visitors.

MONKEY BUSINESS

It seems Arthur was so successful in hiking the sales of Kattomeat, the product he promoted, that the dish was renamed Arthur's in his honour. And there's no doubt that a bunch of animal stars have worked wonders for tea makers Brooke Bond, accelerating sales to the tune of £2 billion. It makes them higher grossing advertising stars than even the likes of superstars Michael Jackson and Madonna.

These animal stars were the unforgettable chimps who slurped PG Tips tea all day long, first making their memorable debut in 1956.

It was on Christmas Day and comedian Peter Sellers spoke for the chimps as they sat having tea in a country house out of dainty china cups on a table laid with silver service.

Later advertisements had them as furniture removers struggling with a piano. When the younger one pipes up: 'Dad, do you know the piano is on my foot?' his father, Mr Shifter, responds with the immortal line: 'You hum it, son, I'll play it.'

Chummy was the chimp who starred in that particular classic. And he was no neanderthal when it came to musical tastes.

Above: *The first PG Tips tea party, filmed in 1956.*

Below: *Mr Shifter.*

The crew tried to substitute a playing piano for one with doctored keys which wouldn't sound a note. Chummy would have nothing to do with it, assuming a policy of non-cooperation until the real thing was supplied.

Then there was the Tour de France cycle race commercial which ended with a worn-out racer pleading: 'Avez-vous un cuppa?' And who can forget the 007 skit which had a chimp as Bond, Brooke Bond?

Other celebrities who did the voices of the chimps include Bob Monkhouse, Su Pollard, Willie Rushton, Cilla Black and Donald Sinden.

The chimpanzees are born in family groups or join one because they have been rejected by their mothers. They are all captive born. The training starts only a few weeks before the shoot date and is fun and entertaining for them. The majority of the actions they do are an extension of their natural playfulness and inquisitiveness. Their reputation for being difficult to work with is unfounded, according to Brooke Bond executive Duncan Bogey: 'We do need to shoot a lot of film but it never takes longer than for humans – about three days.

Their contributions to the success of the advertising is recognized by Brooke Bond with a strict code of practice that guarantees the chimpanzees long-term security in retirement. When they are pensioned off they go to private zoos to be visited regularly by their trainers.

As the years have rolled by, the outcry against using animals for human gain has intensified. Some activists claim the chimps are as outdated a means of advertising as the zoos which cage them. So far, Brooke Bond has no plans to take them off the air.

MR CHATTERBOX

While the voices of the chimps were dubbed, there was one famous animal star who managed his own lines. He was Sparkie, the biggest earning budgie in the world.

Sparkie sprang to prominence in 1958 after being entered in a budgie talking contest by his owner, Mrs Mattie Williams, of Newcastle upon Tyne. She had no idea when she was given the bird as a 6-week-old chick in 1954 that he was something special. When she taught him to say 'pretty Sparkie' in the space of just three weeks she thought he was a standard speaker. But she wasn't prepared for the massive diction he acquired, first under her tuition, then on his own. In total, he mastered 531 words, 383 sentences and eight complete nursery rhymes.

Of course, he won the BBC-run contest and was signed up immediately to advertise a well-known brand of budgie seed on the TV under the new name of 'Mr Chatterbox'. There followed a recording contract and a single was made with Sparkie illustrating the techniques for teaching budgies to talk.

He earned more than £1,000, and had his own bank account and even an income tax number.

When he was 8 years old Sparkie was discovered struggling for breath in the bottom of his cage and died soon afterwards in the loving hands of his owner, just after uttering for the last time: 'I love Mamma'.

Even after death Sparkie remained a celebrity. He was stuffed, mounted on his favourite perch and put in Newcastle's Hancocks Museum with a tape of his incredible nattering.

DYING DOLPHINS

Not all tales of star animals have such a happy ending. Flipper was the world's most famous dolphin after a TV series

captured the imagination of children everywhere.

But the pressures of being a star took its toll. The five captive mammals used for the series were starved to make them perform the necessary tricks. Kathy, the dolphin used most in front of the camera, finally decided she had suffered enough.

One day she caught the eye of her trainer and simply stopped breathing while he held her in his arms. In dolphin terms, she had committed suicide, choosing death rather than prolonged captivity.

It was an experience that scarred the trainer Ric O'Barry. Now he is devoted to releasing all caged dolphins into the wild, where their life span can be up to 40 years instead of the five years that is usual in captivity.

He explains: 'Dolphins only breathe by conscious effort and they can stop living any time they like simply by holding their breath.

'Kathy committed suicide that way, and I am sure many other captive dolphins do – though the reason is always put down as pneumonia or some other stress-related illness.

Above: *Cyril the Cyclist. His catch-phrase –* **avez-vous un cuppa?** *– became a standing joke among schoolchildren the length of Britain.*

SPARKIE'S DYING WORDS WERE FOR HIS LOVING MISTRESS.

'Flipper was both the best thing and the worst thing that ever happened to dolphins. On the one hand she made the public aware of these wonderful animals. On the other, by performing her tricks she allowed the abuse of the animals to become regarded as normal and natural.'

O'Barry went on to establish a haven for dolphins in the Turks and Caicos Islands in the British West Indies.

LASSIE – THE COMPUTER WUFF

Lassie, the wonder dog, has been a firm favourite since he loped on to the screen some 46 years ago, although this blockbusting series brought bad luck for its child star.

Lassie had the uncanny knack of keeping his masters out of trouble not only by averting physical danger but also by deflecting those moral dilemmas which strike at the heart of the young.

His first big screen debut was in 1943 in the film *Lassie Come Home,* alongside Roddy McDowall, Elsa Lanchester and Elizabeth Taylor. He was the dog who made a courageous journey to return to the sides of his loving but poor owners.

There followed a series for TV with Lassie teaming up with Tommy Rettig as loyal owner Jeff Miller. There was plenty of press speculation about the calming influence of the classy canine. But Tommy went on to suffer troubles of his own after his involvement in the series ended when he was just 15. There was a messy divorce case and a conviction for growing marijuana. A prison term for conspiracy to smuggle cocaine was overturned.

It was with some relief then, that Tommy joined the latest series playing Jeff's uncle and even penned some of the scripts.

Every screen Lassie has been trained by the Weatherwax family in the San Fernando Valley of Los Angeles. The last to win the role was the great-great grandson of the original. Nowadays it is not just old-fashioned crooks and collapsing mine shafts that bother the smart collie. He has been taught to grapple with the intricacies of computers in his bid to keep the peace.

Opposite: *Flipper was both the best thing and the worst thing that ever happened to dolphins, claimed his trainer.*

Left: *Lassie with child actor Roddy McDowall. The dog's Big Screen debut came in 1943 with* Lassie Come Home.

Below: *Lassie with his medallion from the Lucky Dog National Canine Defence League.*

THE CAT'S WHISKERS

Fairy-tales are full of stories of Pusses in Boots, but in real life the adventures of our feline friends as they work their way through ten of their nine lives sometimes defy belief.

'Everybody wants to be a cat,' goes the song, and millions of captivated moggy lovers would offer no argument.

Among domestic animals it's hard to think of any that enjoy a cushier life-style. Once they've latched on to a caring owner, found food and a fire, and taunted any resident dogs into submission, they can devote themselves to their greatest love – sleeping.

Yet this popular image is not entirely fair, History shows that some survive well beyond their allotted quota of nine lives and still take life's little risks in their stride.

MOGGY MASCOTS

Cats at war are the classic example. They first seem to have joined up (or rather got themselves conscripted) during the Crimean War of 1854–55.

Captured Russian soldiers would produce helpless little bundles of fur from beneath their greatcoats, kittens they had kept to nurture as best they could until they were old enough to hunt for themselves.

Sometimes the mascot's job went further. Mourka, a tom who saw service with a Russian gun crew during the terrible Battle of Stalingrad in 1942–43, found himself sent on errands across some of the most heavily shelled land in the world.

A message from the battery to HQ would be attached to his collar and Mourka would willingly set off to deliver. Once he had arrived safely – and he managed the run many times – he would be given food and fuss and after a night's rest turned out

Above: *Simon's grave at Ilford, Essex.*

Left: *The Dickin Medal awarded posthumously. Simon remains the only moggy ever to have won the animal equivalent to the VC.*

to find his way back to his comrades at the front.

No one knows what happened to Mourka after the war ended. It seems incredible that he could have survived given the conditions that existed in the city at that time. Yet Russian soldiers who heard of his adventures remained convinced he led a charmed life and insisted he would have lived to enjoy happier times.

Mourka may have had a tough war but

Opposite: *Simon, with one of his shipmates from HMS Amethyst.*

THE CREW WHO HAD SURVIVED THE TERRIBLE ONSLAUGHT WERE AMAZED TO SEE THE BLEEDING CAT STRUGGLE OUT OF THE SHELL-SHATTERED CABIN.

his experiences pale besides those of the Royal Navy's most famous mascot, Simon.

This black-and-white ship's cat, a neutered male, was serving aboard HMS *Amethyst* when the so-called Yangtse Incident erupted in 1949. He'd been handed over as a kitten to the vessel's commanding officer, Lt Cdr Griffiths, a year earlier and was a much loved sight on the ship.

Sailors would always be passing him tasty titbits and he had the freedom of any berth. His rat-catching abilities quickly became legendary and his shipmates would pass the time on a long voyage placing bets on how many dead rats he could produce in a day.

Then the crisis at Nanking boiled up, with the feared army of Red China sweeping aside all resistance which crossed its path. The Chinese captured the Yangtse below Nanking and *Amethyst* was immediately ordered in to protect and evacuate British citizens in the area. Simon was to find himself in the midst of one of the greatest-ever naval adventures.

As the *Amethyst* steamed upriver she came under fire from Chinese batteries on both banks. The ship was struck several times and at last limped on to a sandbank in midstream. When the guns at last fell silent, 54 of her crew were lying dead, dying or seriously injured.

One of the shells had come down on the captain's quarters while Simon was inside as resident guest. The captain died instantly, but amazingly the cat struggled out of the mangled cabin with head and leg injuries and some surface burns. He crawled into a hiding place to lick his wounds and many of the ship's company believed he had quietly gone to find a place to die.

But a few days later he emerged and was soon back at his old rat-catching tricks. This cheered the crew greatly as scores of rats, flushed out by the bombardment, had begun taking over the ship and were causing an enormous health hazard.

Over the next three months Simon played a crucial part in helping keep up the morale of the men. The Chinese had apparently ruled that the ship should not be destroyed, but held prisoner until the right diplomatic conditions were in place for its release.

As the wrangling continued life aboard *Amethyst* was fast becoming unbearable. The weather had been sweltering for weeks, oil stocks were running low and food was becoming fetid. Faced with the choice of staying put to die by disease, or risking the guns, the new commander, Lt Cdr Kerans, decided to make a run for it.

With his engines and hull patched up he headed back downriver under cover of darkness to escape into the South China Sea.

When Simon and his shipmates arrived back in Hong Kong they were given a hero's welcome. The little cat's fame had, by now, been reported around the world and he was showered with presents from a personal fan club.

His story, though, ended on a note of sadness. Simon returned with *Amethyst* to Plymouth for a refit and was taken into quarantine. Three weeks later he was dead, perhaps because he had never fully recovered from the trauma of battle.

To this day Simon remains the only cat ever to have won the Dickin Medal – the animal equivalent of the Victoria Cross. It was presented to him posthumously on 13 April 1950 for his 'meritorious and distinguished service' by the Lord Mayor of Plymouth.

His remains now lie in the People's Dispensary for Sick Animals cemetery at Ilford, Essex.

FEARLESS FELINES

There are many other feline heroes of the waves but two of the most famous this century are the German puss Oscar and an American pet called Maizie.

Oscar, a year-old tabby, was one of several cats aboard *Bismarck* when the ship set sail to wreak havoc among wartime North Atlantic convoys.

When *Bismarck* was finally tracked down by the British fleet and despatched to the bottom of the sea off the French coast, Oscar was plucked out of the waves along with the rest of the German survivors. He joined the crew of the Royal Navy destroyer HMS *Cossack*.

All went well until six months later when *Cossack* was herself torpedoed and sunk. Once again Oscar survived unscathed – this time the aircraft carrier *Ark Royal* was his saviour.

His next life lasted a mere three days. *Ark Royal* was hit by a torpedo in the Mediterranean with heavy loss of life, but though Oscar's chances should have been negligible he somehow clambered on to a piece of wood and was rescued.

After a brief spell in Gibraltar he was found a place in a rest home for old sailors in Northern Ireland, where he lived out his days rather more peacefully. He is likely to remain the only puss ever to escape from three separate shipwrecks.

As for Maizie, she proved how important animals can be to the psychological welfare of humans by propping up the morale of six shipwrecked US sailors whose life raft was set adrift in the Pacific. Maizie stayed alive by eating malted milk tablets and a little water and would move around the laps of each man in turn, licking and comforting them. As one sailor admitted later: 'If Maizie hadn't been with us we might have gone nuts.'

Records show that only one 'civilian' cat has ever won a bravery medal – an attractive female tabby aptly named Faith who moved in to the rectory at St Augustine's Church, next to St Paul's Cathedral.

Just as the Blitz was beginning, with fires erupting around St Paul's, Faith gave birth to a kitten – it was named Panda. The sound of the bombs clearly distressed Faith, but she stayed and could often be seen wandering around the old building as if searching for something. One day the rector understood. He saw her grab Panda from her basket on the top floor and carry him down three flights of stairs to the basement where she'd found a recess containing a pile of old musical scores.

Three days later, on 9 September 1940, a bomb scored a direct hit on the building. Masonry crashed around, fires exploded above her, but throughout it all Faith kept faith. She stayed calm in her hidey-hole, shielding Panda between her front paws, until the noise, dust and smoke subsided. The two cats were found by the rector the next day as he sifted through the ruins, meowing pitifully from the recess where they had been covered by debris.

Both crawled out, dusty but unhurt, and Faith was later awarded a special silver medal by the People's Dispensary for Sick Animals.

Most cat owners can recount tales of how their favourite puss used up at least one of its nine lives, but who can match the performance of a stray called Bonnington (named after the famous British mountaineer Chris Bonnington)?

In February 1980 this moggy got trapped in a dead end with a snarling dog about to pounce for the kill. There was only one escape and it was a sheer climb upwards. Undeterred, Bonnington clawed her way up

THROUGHOUT THE BOMBING RAID SHE SHIELDED HER KITTEN WITH HER FRONT PAWS, AS MASONRY CRASHED DOWN ON THEM AND FIRES EXPLODED ALL AROUND.

Left: *Faith was another feline medal winner. She survived the Blitz on London.*

Below: *Patricia was hurled from the top of the 205 ft St John's Bridge in Portland, Oregon. She survived to become a celebrity.*

Above: *This puss, called Jeremy, got himself stuck at the top of a 65 ft tree in North London.*

THE CAT THOUGHT THE
BRICK KILN WOULD BE A
COSY PLACE TO SPEND THE
WEEKEND; HE WAS RIGHT —
THE TEMPERATURE
REACHED 320°C.

the Bradford block of flats for more than 70 ft before cowering in a gap just below the roof. She was later rescued by an RSPCA man who concluded the pebble-dashed walls of the building had provided just enough grip for the incredible climb.

A similar drama was recorded in Bolton three years later when an inquisitive ginger tom made it to the top of a 150 ft chimney up an old access ladder. He couldn't, however, work out the way down and had to cling on in howling winds for almost a day and a half before he was spotted and rescued.

Sometimes cats with Bonnington-type tendencies don't want to be rescued. One such, called Mincho, ran up a 40 ft tree and stayed there quite happily for six years. Locals in Buenos Aires would push food up to her on the end of a pole and a friendly local milkman made daily deliveries. During her self-imposed exile she even produced three litters – presumably the local toms considered a climb up the tree was well worth their trouble.

PARACHUTING PUSSES

Mincho doesn't quite fall into the miraculous escapes category, but a ginger tom called Gros Minou certainly does ... quite literally. Gros, owned by a Canadian surgeon, fell from the 20th-floor balcony of her master's Outremont penthouse, and plunged more than 200 feet into a flower bed. To the utter disbelief of her vet she survived with little more than a fractured pelvis. Within a week she was crawling again and later made a full recovery.

Other famous fallers include a tom called Pussycat who plunged 120 ft from an 11th-floor flat in London's Maida Vale in 1965. He suffered a broken leg and some internal damage but was soon back to full fitness and was later made a life member of the British Parachute Association.

Then there was perhaps the most celebrated moggy plunger of all – a pregnant puss called Patricia. She survived a fall of around 205 ft after she was hurled off the top of the St John's Bridge in Portland, Oregon, by a heartless motorist. Patricia spent several minutes in the freezing waters of the Willamett River before she was hauled out shocked and bedraggled by two fishermen who were,

appropriately enough, out to catch catfish. They must have gone home with the tallest angler's tale in history.

That night Patricia aborted two of her kittens but an exploratory operation by a vet found that although all her organs were severely bruised there was no life-threatening injury. Patricia was later adopted by local cat lovers Fritz and Mardi Jacob and went on to make numerous star guest appearances at cat shows across America.

Studies have shown that falling cats reach their maximum speed of 40 mph after about 60 ft. In theory, this should mean that if it's possible for them to survive a 200 ft fall it's also possible for them to handle 2,000 ft or more. Thankfully the theory never seems to have been put to the test.

NINE LIVES?

There are plenty of other examples of cats cheating death just as they seemed to be shuffling off this mortal coil. One of the most bizarre accounts came from Cambridgeshire, England, when a tom called Sedgewick decided to make an electricity substation part of his territory. He could hardly have made a bigger mistake.

As his paw touched a live wire he received a 33,000-volt shock which blacked out more than 40,000 homes. Yet, incredibly, a seriously singed Sedgewick recovered consciousness sufficiently to drag himself 60 ft back to the home of his owner, a Mr Ray Hammond. Mr Hammond could hardly recognize his pet – he later likened Sedgewick to a burnt-out car tyre – but after suitable care from a vet the chastened cat was soon back to his old self.

There are loads more from the feline mould which produced Sedgewick. Like the cat which once accidentally got itself shut in a brick kiln in Minerva, Ohio, on Friday evening and actually made it out alive the following Monday despite temperatures approaching 320°C.

And what about the one which got itself buried in tons of cement for more than two days? It had been looked after by labourers working on a new cultural centre in Skopje, Yugoslavia, but suddenly vanished on the day they were setting up planks to mould a new wall.

When the wood was later pulled off, the cat was found embedded in the concrete and had somehow kept breathing by squeezing its nose through a crack in the boards. The impression its body left was preserved and became a popular tourist attraction.

There are three other documented reports of cats disproving the old adage that curiosity will always make an end of them. The first dates back to 1955 when a painfully thin puss was found in a packing case full of car components at Natal in South Africa.

The case had been sealed up at the old Morris car works in Cowley, England, in August – three months earlier – and the cat had stayed alive by eating an instruction manual and licking engine oil. She was rushed to a vet but died the following day.

A happier ending was recorded in Cairo when a puss was pulled out of a diesel engine crate which had been sealed up 41 days earlier in Detroit, Michigan. She had also lived on engine grease and, though thin, it had kept her in good enough condition to give birth to four kittens. The entire family was nursed back to health and later thrived.

Then there was a tabby called Thumper which belonged to a Westminster woman. Thumper was fascinated by the workings of the lift to her home but somehow contrived to get herself stuck at the bottom of the shaft. Her owner assumed she had wandered off and got run over, until passengers in the lift detected her pitiful meows from the basement. She was rescued after more than seven weeks on a diet of oily water, but never quite recovered and eventually had to be put to sleep.

Bearing in mind that most cats hate water, the most miserable ordeal of all was endured by a 3-year-old called Peter. He was pulled out of the wreck of a ship called the *Tjoba* when it capsized and sank in the River Rhine in 1964. Peter kept going for an amazing eight days under water by keeping his head and whiskers inside a tiny air pocket.

WILDCAT STRIKES

's this uncanny knack for survival that ends to mark cats out among most household pets. Perhaps their genetic make-up means that, even today, they are not so very far removed from their cousins, the big cats. Given half a chance they can quickly adapt to going native.

Proof of this is emerging across the globe. Captive-bred animals such as lynxes, pumas, black panthers and jungle cats have shown they can keep themselves alive in unfamiliar country, even though it was always thought they would lack the necessary hunting skills.

Above: *One of the mysterious big cats now repopulating Britain's wilder regions. This one was shot in Scotland in 1983.*

Left: *The cast of a big cat's paw mark made after a farmer saw the animal in Devon, England. The paw measures 5 in across.*

THE BEAST OF EXMOOR
HAUNTS THE BLEAK
MOORLANDS, SLAUGHTERING
SHEEP AND EVADING
CAPTURE WITH FELINE
CUNNING.

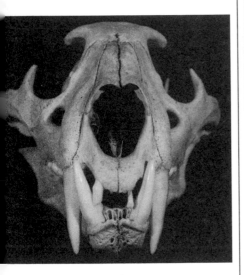

Above: *The skull of a big cat, thought to be the size of a lion, found on Dartmoor, Devon, in 1988.*

Above right: *Ship's cat from the* Cutty Sark, *berthed in London.*

In England, sightings of wildcats are becoming increasingly common. The so-called Beast of Exmoor, which slaughtered sheep for years on the bleak moorland which is one of England's last wildernesses, has been seen by too many witnesses (including police) to be a figment of imagination.

And in Shropshire scientists have been given even better evidence – the body of what is thought to have been a jungle cat. This animal, which is not native to Britain or Europe, was found by farmer Norman Evans in 1989 near his home. It seems to have been knocked down by a car and died of starvation because of its subsequent inability to hunt.

Forensic tests later showed it had probably been living wild for up to five years after escaping from some private collection. Despite its distinctive short, black-ringed tail, the stripes on its limbs and its terrifying inch-long fangs, it had managed to keep itself away from prying human eyes with outstanding success.

Though bigger captive-bred cats, such as panthers and pumas, can and do support themselves after escaping into the countryside, it is unlikely that they would ever get the chance to breed. Interbreeding between these animals is rare, and their offspring are almost always sterile.

That's why the future for wild jungle cats is so fascinating. They can breed successfully with feral animals, the closest relative to domestic cats, and their offspring remain fully fertile.

According to one of the world's leading experts on cat hybrids, cryptozoologist Karl Shuker, it is possible that in Britain and many other countries around the world wildcats are emerging as permanent wildlife residents.

He says: 'There is a realistic chance that interbreeding between escapee jungle cats, leopard cats, and feral domestic cats has begun in Britain's countryside.

'If this continues, eventually a self-perpetuating strain of notably large hybrids could become established here – hybrids, moreover, that possess genes from a wild non-native species unlike the hybrids produced by interbreeding between feral domestic cats and the native Scottish wildcat.

'The result would be a startling feline parallel to the cross-breeding between native red deer and naturalized Asian sika deer – and an unpredictable addition to the British ecosystem.'

Perhaps the biggest single difference between domestic cats and the escapees is the way they each regard home. Whereas the wilder feline will happily roam hundreds of miles to hunt, domestic moggies positively hate moving off their established territory.

PUSSY FOOTING IT

In past centuries it was always considered unlucky to make a cat 'do a flit' – move from one property to another. This was partly because of a cat's reputation as a witch's familiar. Perceived wisdom suggested one should avoid upsetting the animal at all costs.

Consequently there are countless stories of cats overcoming unlikely odds to return to areas they regard as home. One of the greatest feats was accomplished by a little Australian tom named Silky who was taken with his owners on a caravan holiday about 200 miles north of Brisbane. On the first night Silky was allowed out to have a wander round but he immediately vanished and a search failed to find any trace of him. Owner Ken Philips and his family hoped against hope he would turn up during the holiday but he never did and they reluctantly made the 1,481-mile trek home to Melbourne, Victoria, without him.

Nine months later, however, Silky reappeared on the doorstep of their home. He was exhausted and half-starved, but seemed to have coped with his journey well. It was only after he had settled down again for a few days that the enormous physical strain of the journey seemed to catch up with him. A week after his miracle reappearance he died.

Even more extraordinary is the story of a cream-coloured Persian cross called Sugar. His owners, a Mr and Mrs Woods, had to leave him with a helpful neighbour when they decided to retire from their house in Anderson, California, to a farm in Oklahoma.

Sugar was terrified of cars and even being carried near one threw him into a panic. Transporting him for more than 1,500 miles was unthinkable. The Woods thought they had said goodbye to their pet for ever, but one morning 13 months later a cat looking suspiciously like Sugar suddenly hopped on to Mrs Woods's back as she bent to do some weeding.

Above: *This pampered puss was left a fortune when her owner died – ensuring luxury to the end of her days.*

Left: *The best-protected cat in London. This moggy got herself adopted by the Life Guards of the Royal Household.*

IN AN EFFORT TO CURB HIS WANDERLUST HIS OWNER EVEN DOSED HIM WITH THE CONTRACEPTIVE PILL.

At first she refused to believe it could be her old cat but as she stroked the 'stranger' she found his hip joint had the same peculiarity that had troubled Sugar for many years. A phone call to her former neighbour confirmed the startling fact that the cat had somehow tracked them down.

If some pussies are expert navigators, others seem to have almost been bred as marathon moggies. In 1960 a tabby called McCavity scampered from Glasgow back to his old home in Truro, Cornwall, in an incredible three weeks. That meant he covered the 500 miles at the rate of almost 24 miles a day. Sadly, the effort killed him. The day after he arrived back a neighbour found him and gave him milk but he was already too exhausted to drink it.

Three years later an even more remarkable case surfaced in South Africa. A 12-year-old tom managed to cover the 700 miles between Johannesburg and Port Elisabeth (his old home) in only ten days. Seventy miles a day sounds hard to believe but the other possibilities are even less convincing.

It wasn't as though the cat was a tug-of-love case, in which the losing owner had gone to fetch him. So how did he manage it? Hitch-hike?

Just as there are fast cats, there are slow and persistent ones. The slowest tracker on record was a lovely Siamese called Ching. She toddled off from a caravan site at Ammanford, South Wales, in 1967 to find the family home back at Stow-on-the-Wold in Gloucestershire. It took her three years, which works out at a less-than-impressive rate of 175 yards a day.

The prize for persistence, on the other hand, has to go to a Persian cross named BC who in 1979 was so irritated at being moved out of his comfortable home in Palmerston North, New Zealand, that he made it his mission in life to return. So return he did. Seventy-eight times, in fact. The journey may only have been two miles but there were at least four main roads in between and countless others where he could have fallen foul of cars.

His owner, Mrs Marjorie Cummerfield, tried everything she could think of to stop him. She once ambushed him in mid-route, but that only made him more watchful the next time he escaped. She even followed a vet's advice to give him hormone treatment in the form of the contraceptive pill. It may have done wonders for BC's hormones but it did nothing for his wanderlust.

Amazingly BC survived the perils of 20th-century transport to die peacefully of natural causes in 1983.

Mother-love is perhaps the strongest emotion of all in cats (in common with the rest of us) and there can be no better mum than a puss owned by a Manhattan family. They took her out to a summer house 100 miles away in the countryside for a few idyllic months. The plan certainly suited puss, for she quickly became pregnant, and when it was time to leave she vamooshed.

Her owners returned to New York resigned to losing her for ever. Then, three months later, she appeared from nowhere carrying a kitten in her mouth – clearly determined that the little one should grow up in the city with a family that could be loved and trusted.

The celebration was hardly under way though when she again did a bunk, leaving the kitten behind. Two weeks passed and just as hope was again fading up she popped again ... with another kitten between her teeth. Her owners needed no more clues as to what was going on. They packed cat and kittens in the car and headed back to the sticks to find the rest of the litter to save mum the trouble of running a complete shuttle service.

Pussy-footing is OK for some, but the

Below: *Lucky the cat survived nine weeks inside a crate being shipped from the UK to Texas. Here British Caledonian staff prepare to fly him home.*

more discerning moggy travellers find that what's good enough for humans is good enough for them. Take air travel. One of the most extraordinary journeys ever recorded of the animal kingdom happened in the spring of 1979 when a Siamese called Wan Ton somehow hopped on to a jumbo jet from Guam in the south Pacific.

He was found in the hold of the jet by staff at London Heathrow, shivering and looking extremely sorry for himself. There was just one problem for the British authorities as they quarantined Wan Ton ready to return him to the American naval family which owned him. No plane flew from that part of the world direct to London. Somehow, Wan Ton had changed planes at Washington DC.

Another seasoned air traveller was Hamlet, a cat owned by one Paul Rackheath of Norfolk. In February 1984 he was on the official passenger list of a BA jumbo flying out of Toronto, but he obviously didn't like the menu because he escaped from his cage and vanished into the hold.

It wasn't until two months later that a startled aircraft engineer caught sight of a thin, scrawny scrap of fur behind some panelling. He pulled out Hamlet, who had apparently survived by licking condensation. Though he didn't know it, the hapless feline had flown around 600,000 miles in a little over seven weeks, including stopovers in Jamaica, Singapore, Australia and Kuwait.

Finally, there is the not quite so traumatic but every bit as uncomfortable story of Buttons, a 'lucky' black cat from Great Yarmouth, England.

He vanished one afternoon at exactly the time as his owner's next-door-neighbour set off from home to drive to Aberdeen. Being a sensible sort of motorist, the driver, a Mr Fraser Robertson, decided to pull in to a service station to check his oil. As he lifted the bonnet he instantly spied Buttons curled up around the battery and absolutely covered in thick engine grime.

As Mr Robertson observed later: 'How she survived six hours of non-stop driving I will never know.

'The engine was incredibly hot and what with the petrol fumes, the oil smoke and the noise it must have been a terrifying experience for her.'

Fortunately things got better for Buttons. She got a quick bite at the service station and was then driven on to Aberdeen with the luxury of being able to curl up on the back seat.

Best of all, one airline gave her a free flight home.

Left: *They may have nine lives but it still helps to have the Royal Society for the Prevention of Cruelty to Animals on their side.*

Below: *American puss Shandy became the only cat in the world to eat her dinner with chopsticks!*

UNDER THE SEA

The leviathans of the mysterious deeps are a symbol of nature's power and greatness, but some people will pursue even these majestic creatures and subject them to cruel ordeals in their insatiable lust for money.

For many they are the symbol of nature's greatness: the sight of whales roaming the oceans unfettered and free is a reminder that the world still has giants on the loose. Yet also they are a poignant sign of human power misused. The majestic mammals which should have been cherished have been threatened by greed.

As fishing fleets sought to spear or net whales to profit from their meat and oils, their numbers dwindled to the point of extinction. Just in time, the world woke up to its folly. Commercial whaling was banned – although controversy still rages about the issue – and the seas seemed at last a little safer for these graceful creatures.

At a time when whales had earned a special place in the hearts of wildlife lovers, one in particular captured the imagination of the West as it strove to escape from its Russian masters.

KILLER WHALES?

Brightness the beluga whale was a reluctant volunteer in the Russian Navy, one of several whales and dolphins in captivity at a Black Sea laboratory in Sebastopol, trained for dangerous missions under the waves.

Special underwater agents like Brightness have been used by America and Russia for the past 30 years. They were in action against Vietcong frogmen during America's involvement in the Vietnam conflict. So valuable were they that Russian

Opposite: *A white beluga whale, similar to Brightness, makes friends with a diver in the Black Sea.*

Below: *Brightness was eventually caught by his Russian masters, despite worldwide protests. Here he is winched unceremoniously aboard a trawler.*

Above: *Brightness lies helpless on his makeshift stretcher – sedated for the long voyage back to captivity.*

THE FRIENDLY FUGITIVE EVEN MANAGED BROAD SMILES FOR THE CAMERA.

Right: *Movie director Michael Winner vowed to raise £100,000 to buy Brightness from the Russians.*

fishermen were paid a ransom for supplying live beluga whales.

Taking advantage of their amiable personality and sharp wit, scientists trained them to stick limpet mines or listening devices on submarines or ships and even kill enemy divers with a syringe attached to their noses. Diving swiftly to enormous depths and impervious to the cold, the whale seemed a perfect antidote to the menace of enemy submarines. They were even taught to distinguish different metals. But stealth alone would not save them from certain death in their explosives work. Clearly visible thanks to their bright white skins, they would be easy targets in times of war. Theirs would almost certainly be kamikaze missions.

Few people realized lovable whales and dolphins were being trained for warfare even though an estimated 100 were caged for the purpose in Russia alone. Then Brightness made a bid for freedom. It happened in November 1991 when a winter storm lashed at the Black Sea coast. The wind whipped up a sea strong enough to tear down the cages which penned Brightness and his buddy Gorgeous.

For several months Brightness enjoyed a freedom in the waves he had never known before, but it seems he missed the human companionship he had grown used to in captivity. He turned up off the Turkish coast, 500 miles from where he disappeared. Fishermen and tourists alike were treated to regular displays of his antics off the village

of Gerze. He would allow admirers to pet and feed him. Soon the eyes of the world were on the frolicking, feted creature who even managed broad smiles for the cameras.

But it was the start of an international battle over his future between Russia and the West. Both sides agreed the waters of the Black Sea would become too warm for the fugitive whale to survive as the summer hotted up. Russians insisted the creature should be returned to them, claiming he was being trained for circus work. Brightness was never used for military purposes, insisted the Leningrad Scientific Research Institute, and would perish in the icy waters of the Arctic, his natural habitat. In fact, he depended on the close human contact he had grown to know and had been wasting away while he was at sea, it was claimed.

In Britain, scorn was poured on the news that Brightness was anything other than a pawn in the Cold War games played by the superpowers. Claims that he was being prepared for a life as a circus attraction led to an outcry. Furious campaigners claimed the only place fit for the whale was the open sea. Britain's Whale and Dolphin Conservation Society hurriedly assembled a team of experts to assess the best course of action. An airlift to the Arctic was on the cards. 'We have no doubt it could survive there', declared director Sean Whyte.

But as the freedom fighters were

mobilizing their forces, the Russians acted. For an hour Brightness ducked and dived, thwarting their attempts at capture. But finally the 900 lb creature was lassoed around the tail by a diver and hauled aboard a specially adapted trawler to be carted back unceremoniously in a heavyweight sling. Before the 120-mile journey back to Russian territory and a two-day journey to the Sebastopol base, he was sedated. For once, Brightness – whose Russian name Tishka means 'laughing man' – had lost the by-now familiar beam. Instead, the 7-year-old whale looked glum and despairing.

Politicians declined to intervene because of the sensitive nature of the issue, but the row refused to go away. Revelations that 13 ft long Brightness was to star in a travelling marine show touring the holiday hotspots in a floating cage further outraged conservationists. Dr Boris Zhurid, director of the Aquamarine Dolphinarium in Sebastopol, described how the sea-borne cage comprising three swimming pools was to be pulled by a tug.

There was no comfort, either, for those who sought freedom for Brightness in the knowledge that an American oceanarium keen to begin breeding beluga whales in captivity was prepared to pay £100,000 to the hard-up Russians and import Brightness as a celebrity to its 170,000 sq ft pool, already home to two belugas and four dolphins.

British star Paul McCartney, TV writer Carla Lane and film producer Michael Winner pledged to raise £100,000 so they could buy the whale and release him back into the wild. But their attempts failed.

Just two months after he was harnessed off Turkey, Brightness was performing in a show, doing tricks such as singing, waving his fins and fetching balls.

But the clowning, grinning animal who had so beguiled the world was gone, his spirit numbed by the cheerless monotony of life in the ring.

Thanks to pressure from Turkey, the Russians were ready to release Brightness into the waters where he first tasted freedom, to recuperate. British rescuers then negotiated a way of freeing Brightness and fellow captive Yegor after a lengthy rehabilitation process. There was jubilation among the conservationists who wanted him free.

However, between them, nature and the

whale who refused to be caged had other ideas. History repeated itself when a violent storm wrecked the netting which held Brightness. One dolphin was killed and another, along with Yegor the whale, was seriously hurt. Despite an alert put out along the coastline, Brightness disappeared, choosing the depths of the Black Sea to swim in and only coming up occasionally for air. Soviet news agency TASS offered a £400 reward for the creature, describing him as a state asset. There were fears he could have been killed by pollution or even starved to death.

Above: *Brightness makes his triumphant return to the Black Sea port of Gerze, Turkey, in April 1993.*

THE ESKIMOS COULD NOT BEAR TO SEE SUCH NOBLE CREATURES BLOODIED AND BATTERED AS THEY TRIED TO FORCE A PATH THROUGH THE FROZEN SEAS.

It was four months before Brightness was spotted, in April 1993, safe and well and making himself at home once again in the waters off the Turkish coast. He came up to give free shows, to the delight of the Turkish crowds which gathered. But bitterly aware of his previous encounters, he refused to stay long enough to be caught. As far as anyone knows, Brightness is still enjoying freedom, somewhere under the waves in the Black Sea.

A CAGE OF ICE

It was the plight of whales in peril which focused the attention of the world in 1988. This time Russia and America were united in their efforts to free three whales trapped by ice in the Arctic.

The trio of Californian greys had become trapped after lingering too long in the sea at Barrow, Alaska, before migrating south in the face of unusually cold weather. The winter ice closed in relentlessly around them.

It was the Eskimos living in the darkened, snowy wastes of the north who first realized the appalling predicament of the whales. They witnessed the increasingly desperate animals becoming bashed and bloodied as they tried to force a path through the unyielding crust of ice that caged them.

The Eskimos live by hunting whales, but even they could not bear to see the grand animals die such a cruel death, being suffocated by snow.

In rotas, they used picks and saws to make life-saving air holes in the 2 ft thick ice, each one closer to the sea, now some five miles distant. Each whale was given a pet name: they were Pouto, Siku and Kannick, meaning Ice Hole, Ice and Snowflake. To keep one 20 ft by 24 ft breathing hole open meant men working in relays for a week. Their endeavours were screened on American TV and the nation watched with bated breath to see if the animals would make it.

Soon oil workers, members of Greenpeace, national guardsmen and biologists joined the army intent on freeing the whales. Each day the open sea was getting further away as the big winter freeze got a grip.

In temperatures of minus 13°C during the day and with winds peaking at 30 mph, the volunteers were clad in special heavy-duty parkas, insulated trousers, vacuum-lined boots and even facemasks to protect them against the biting cold. Their reward was a bond which sprang up between beast and man, based on trust and a shared hope. It was enough to make grown men endure until they were on the point of collapse.

One of the whales was 30 ft long and thought to be about 6 years old. The others were smaller, probably aged only about 2.

Right: *Californian grey whales battle for survival after being cut off by advancing ice north of Alaska. Volunteers worked around the clock to keep their air holes open. The whales were freed ... but no one knows whether they survived to reach breeding grounds.*

It was clear that more high-tech methods would be needed if the whales were to stand any chance at all. Initial hopes lay in an effective ice-crushing hovercraft barge which would pulverize the ice and open an escape route for the whales. Normally used for transporting supplies to oil drilling sites, it was based 200 miles away and time was crucial. A giant helicopter was ready to hoist the 185-ton machine to the scene.

But jagged icebergs posed a threat to the air cushion on which the ice cutter travelled before it even approached Barrow. The whales had been trapped for more than two weeks before the steel-tipped concrete block began punching holes at 75 yd spaces towards the trapped animals.

For one it was already too late. The smallest of the three lost his struggle for life. To the consternation of the army of rescuers, he failed to surface one morning and the whale the American-speaking observers had called Bone was pronounced lost. He was severely weakened after the skin on his snout had been worn away against the ice, exposing the bone beneath. The remaining two, known as Crossbeak and Bonnet to the Americans, continued their bleak course from air hole to air hole.

Other dangers were now threatening. Hungry polar bears had picked up the scent of whales in trouble. Several were closing in for a kill, having already claimed the life of a whale trapped further down the coast. If they decided to attack, there was little the onlookers could do. There arose the spectre of the whales, the centre of media attention from all over the world, being eaten alive as the cameras rolled.

Then there was the question of cost. The rescue operation was gobbling up money to the tune of some $1 million. Critics began braving the public obsession with the freedom of the whales. Could not the money have been better spent on the nation's homeless or sick?

Scientists weighed in with their doubts as well. Exhausted as they were by their fight against the ice, the whales were surely unlikely to survive the trip down to the warmer waters of Mexico where others of their kind were beginning to mate. There were sharks to contend with off the shores of British Columbia, too.

Fortunately for the trapped whales,

America's President Reagan and President Gorbachev from the USSR didn't agree. Distracted though he was with a presidential election at home, President Reagan, like most of his country, found the battle for survival off the northern tip of his territory compelling.

And he seized on an offer by the Soviet president of two ice breakers to churn up a path for the whales. The Soviets could already boast of some success in freeing whales. In 1985 they lured nearly 1,000 white whales from beneath ice in the Bering Sea, playing classical music underwater to soothe the petrified creatures.

Only 40 died and the Russians were confident they could repeat their achievement. Finally, following the ship *Vladimir Arseniev*, the two whales reached seas free of the icy shackles which had harnessed them for three weeks.

Below: *Dolphins love to play alongside boats, leaping to catch the odd morsel of food. Though gentle to human beings, they can turn into raging fighters when confronted by sharks.*

*Above: **Pacific bottlenose dolphins at play.***

WOULD THE WHALES REACH THE SAFETY OF WARMER WATERS — OR WOULD THEY PERISH?

---

*Below: **Fungie the dolphin frolics with divers.***

distress of the whales. They realized that with the world backing the whales, it would be too devastating for the countless well-wishers if the whales didn't make it. As for the previous three weeks, hope was all everybody had.

Blue whales are the largest mammals to have inhabited the Earth. They have been recorded with lengths of up to 108 ft and weights of up to an astonishing 131 tons. Swimming at speed, they can reach 14 knots. Even baby blues are a force to be reckoned with: they can measure 25 ft on arrival with a weight of more than 7 tons. In 1932 the tongue of an 89 ft long whale weighed in at a mind-boggling 3 tons 3 cwt.

THE DANCE OF THE DOLPHINS

A message was flashed simultaneously to Presidents Reagan and Gorbachev. It was hailed as a meaningful accord between the two superpowers with a history of antagonism. The US president sent a message of personal thanks to everyone involved in the feat. 'It's an inspiring endeavour. The human persistence and determination of many individuals on behalf of these whales shows mankind's concern for the environment.'

No one knows the eventual fate of the whales: whether they reached the safety of warmer waters or died in the fight to get there.

Scientists in the frontline of the rescue could easily have monitored their progress by attaching radio transmitters to them but decided against it. It wasn't just that they were concerned that it would add to the

With their might and grandeur, whales are surely the rulers under the waves, but they have to go a long way to pip the dolphin in the popularity stakes. Perhaps it is the dolphins' cheeky, toothy grin or a warmth which radiates out of the coldest of waters. Above all, they appear to revel in human companionship.

Naturalist Sir David Attenborough explains: 'They have a justifiable reputation for helping man. Possibly it is because we are approximately the same size and they feel they are helping others of their own kind.'

Next to humans, dolphins have the largest and most complex brains in the animal kingdom.

Above all, they love to help children, perhaps sensing they are the least able to

help themselves. That's why they are used in Miami in therapy for autistic children.

In 1988 three children were rescued by a caring dolphin after they were thrown from a blazing ferry by their father into the sea off Java. The gentle creature used his nose to guide them to a waiting life raft.

Surfer Adam Maguire was quite literally saved from the jaws of death by dolphins after he was attacked by a shark off the coast of New South Wales, Australia.

The 17-year-old had been larking about with some pals and a school of dolphins when a 13 ft killer shark struck. As it tried to take a bite out of the schoolboy, three gallant dolphins intervened. They butted and bashed the attacker until it gave up and swam off.

Afterwards Adam, from Ballina, Brisbane, said: 'We were out and there was a school of dolphins around. We were just mucking around with them. They were catching waves with us.

'Then I saw what appeared to be a dolphin charging towards me. But 5 metres away I realized it was a shark. By then it was too late and I was knocked off my board. Then the shark came back again and hit me.

'I just tried to push it away and then I saw it swim off. As it left, I saw three dolphins chasing it away.'

Two shipwrecked sailors were nudged to safety through shark-infested waters off Indonesia by a school of dolphins. A Dutch helicopter pilot also owes his life to a sea-borne saviour. After he crashed in the sea in the Far East a dolphin pushed his life raft for nine days until they reached land.

The argument that dolphins are better friends to mankind than even a dog has been disputed by scientists who reckon they would probably act to save themselves and their young rather than any human victim.

Yet Dr Horace Dobbs, a former scientist at Harwell, Oxfordshire, found himself reassessing his views on dolphins after he saw one swim beneath his 13-year-old son in waters off the Isle of Man and provide a ride around the bay. The experience prompted him to write a book, *Dance to a Dolphin's Song*, and convinced him that swimming with the animals was a cure for depression. 'I felt I had to know more about creatures with such a closeness to man. The best way to teach a dog is to reward him with food but dolphins aren't interested in bribery. They are motivated by love. If a trainer turns his back on a dolphin it feels badly rejected.'

Ask any of the residents around Dingle Bay in Ireland and they will give dolphins a glowing reference. That's where Fungi the dolphin has set up home, to the delight of residents and tourists alike. They cram themselves into small boats and head out to sea to watch his playful antics. Ted Kennedy Junior, son of Senator Teddy Kennedy, was one of thousands who travelled across the world and Ireland to be captivated by the flip-flap frolics in the water.

Fungi became the star of several films, including a documentary called *The Dolphin's Gift*, narrated by actor John Hurt.

Likewise, on the bleak north-east coast of Britain, Jimmy the dolphin made himself at home in the harbour of Amble to the

Above: *A school of southern right whale dolphins assemble off the Chilean coast. The mammal's close relationship with mankind is the stuff of legend – yet there are still fishermen who cruelly hunt them to obtain the 'aphrodisiac' dorsal fin.*

THIS BARBAROUS PRACTICE LEAVES THE DOLPHIN BLEEDING TO DEATH AND SPIRALLING OUT OF CONTROL INTO THE DEPTHS OF THE OCEAN.

Right: *This killer shark caught off Miami in 1972 had preyed on swimmers in local waters. Its razor-like teeth enabled it to kill in seconds.*

Below: *A great white shark, the model for the monster in the hit movie* Jaws.

surprise and joy of the locals. Flatteringly, he appears to stay because he wants to, not because he needs to.

Sadly, however, there are people who will happily line their own pockets at the expense of even the closest animal ally.

Dolphins are slaughtered wholesale by unscrupulous tuna fishermen when they become trapped in mammoth drag nets which are trawled through the seas.

Even more appallingly, a trade in dolphin fins has sparked a barbarous practice. It began when *Science* magazine branded dolphins as 'promiscuous as Errol Flynn'. Apparently, desperate Japanese men believed crushed dorsal fin from the sexually active creature would be a cure-all for their own sexual inadequacies.

It has prompted greedy fishermen off the Japanese and Australian coasts to haul dolphins aboard their boats, hack off the desired fin and ditch the body back into the sea, alive, bleeding profusely and spiralling out of control into the depths of the ocean.

There are rich pickings for fishermen, who can sell the fin for £1,000 a time. Although they risk imprisonment and a hefty fine, there's little chance of them ever being caught.

It was this horrible fate that befell Charlie, a friendly dolphin from the waters of Shark Bay, Western Australia. After

being speared by a fishing hook, Charlie beached himself, hoping for some human aid. It came and cheerful Charlie repaid the kindness of the passing fisherman by driving fish into his net. He was a firm favourite with all the local people, particularly the children. But this trusting and loyal creature was killed by the ruthless fin fishermen.

In his honour, a dolphin sanctuary was formed and is home to scores of dolphins who will happily play and prance in the water with visiting families.

People can enter the water safe in the knowledge that the dolphins will see off any marauding shark, one of the most feared creatures on Earth.

THE JAWS OF DEATH

Sharks have always posed a threat in the water, but the 1975 film *Jaws* – masterly in its suspense although criticized for its unrealistic monster model – moulded the paranoia of a generation.

And it may be that just such a beast existed after a spate of attacks along America's east coast in July 1916, thought to be the work of one rogue creature. Four people died and another was injured at a time when it was widely believed sharks did not attack bathers in the safer northern waters – while perhaps large mackerel or turtles might. In the first attack, the shark was so tenacious it clamped onto its

victim's leg in as little as 18 in of water.

Four days later and 35 miles farther north another man died. Within the week, two more people died and another was savagely injured after the shark entered a sheltered creek 20 miles from the open sea. President Woodrow Wilson summoned his advisors in a bid to curb the menace while shark hunters took to the water.

It was only days before a great white measuring 8.5 ft was hooked; its stomach contained a mass of flesh and bone. When the attacks ended, it was assumed this was the shark responsible for all the killings.

Possibly the worst shark attack in recent years came in June 1993 when a 34-year-old British woman was eaten alive by a 16 ft long shark during a dive.

The 2-ton great white shark – the same breed which terrorized the resort in *Jaws* – attacked moments after Therese Cartwright went into the water with two other divers, intending to study seal pups in a colony off the coast of Tasmania, Australia.

The shark probably mistook Mrs Cartwright, aged 34, for one of the seals it normally feasts on. Mrs Cartwright was mother to quadruplets born in 1987 following fertility treatment and also to an 11-month-old son. They were in an escort boat with her husband Ian when the shark attacked. The family had left their native Kent for a new life in Australia and midwife Mrs Cartwright was on the point of qualifying for a Master's degree.

In the same week bride Debbie Ford watched as her husband was eaten alive by an 18 ft great white shark. The couple had been married for only three weeks.

Victim John Ford was diving off the New South Wales resort of Byron Bay when the monster loomed. Fishermen gave chase but the shark was so powerful it dragged a trawler 4 miles out to sea before breaking out of its nets. Experts deemed it unlikely that the same fish was responsible for both deaths.

There have been 491 shark attacks around the Australian coastline since the first was recorded in 1792, 182 of them being fatal.

That is an average of two a year.

But even the awesome great white is suffering at human hands. Although they are not a protected species, there are thought to be as few as 2,000 remaining

worldwide. Despite their menace, biologists want the numbers conserved because of their important role in the ecosystem.

The largest of the sharks is the rare whale shark. It is a peaceable enough fish but it averages 50 ft in length and weighs 15 tons. One baby examined by scientists had a liver weighing 600 lb and 3,000 teeth in each of its jaws. The whale shark also has the unnerving habit of scratching its back on the bottom of boats, with quite frightening consequences.

Sometimes even a shark meets its match, however. Kelly Rafferty, a 38-year-old fisherman, fell overboard in shark-filled waters off Cairns, Australia, in May 1992. But Kelly wasn't about to become breakfast for any passing fish. He described his 9-mile swim to safety. 'I slapped a 12 ft tiger shark out of the road, got some stingers out of my feet and punched a 4 ft Java shark on the way to shore.' Doctors who treated him in hospital said afterwards he was in good condition despite the ordeal.

Above: *A shark ends its fight for survival as fishermen in South Australian waters haul it aboard their boat.*

EACH OF ITS POWERFUL JAWS CONTAINS 3,000 VICIOUS TEETH.

THE STARS AND
ANIMAL RIGHTS

Imprisoned by fame themselves, it is hardly surprising that many celebrities use their wealth and power to fight for the rights of animals who have no voice.

In the hype-ridden world of showbiz the animal kingdom is, for many stars, the only way truly to escape. Famous faces queue up to defend species at risk with a passion matched only on stage or in front of a camera.

Perhaps it's because the stars get tired of the human hassle – the terms of a new film deal, agents upping their cut or some schmuck trying to sell gossip to the papers.

Whatever the reason, animals suffering abuse get some powerful voices on their side.

And for those lucky enough to be picked as pets of the stars there are luxuries many humans can only dream of.

MONKEY BUSINESS

Take Bubbles the chimp, for instance. Life started as badly as it possibly could for him in the research laboratory of an American company.

Yet just as it seemed he might end up as one more grim statistic of science, along came salvation in the shape of one of the world's best-known singers, Michael Jackson.

Michael rescued Bubbles and gave him new life about as far removed as possible from his job as a living, breathing experiment. There began a love affair as intense as any Hollywood has ever seen.

For six years Bubbles never left Michael's side. He toured with the Jackson entourage, staying in £2,000-a-night hotel suites and living off the finest food.

He even slept next to his master's bed.

Michael would kit him out in the latest designer clothes to make sure he never looked underdressed at the constant round of parties.

And Bubbles, real name *Anthropopithecus*, was once even said to have bathed in Perrier water because Jackson thought it would be purer for his fur.

When Bubbles wasn't on tour he could enjoy the freedom of Michael's Santa Ynez ranch under the care of his personal animal bodyguard Miko Brando, son of Marlon.

Michael, of course, would try to visit daily to play and talk or collect him for

another personal appearance at some star-studded bash. Sadly, however, that close relationship had to end.

Male chimps are known to have terrible tempers. At 160 lb, Bubbles easily had the muscle-power to kill a man.

Reluctantly Michael agreed his favourite pet would have to retire to a private zoo at Sylmar, Los Angeles. And although Bubbles lost a little of his freedom, love, care and the company of other chimps helped him to settle in quickly.

Bubbles's friendship with Michael is typical of relationships that many stars enjoy with the animal kingdom.

Famous actors and singers will tell time and again how they trust animals more than humans, and talk of the need to stand up for creatures defenceless against the ravages of mankind.

Opposite: *Liz Taylor and her former husband Richard Burton had a weakness for cute, hairy dogs.*

Above: *Michael Jackson with his pet chimp Bubbles and friend. Bubbles got used to the luxury of £2,000-a-night hotels.*

ONCE SHE LAVISHED HER CARE AND ATTENTION ON MEN; NOW HER LOVE IS GIVEN TO STRAY CATS AND DOGS.

BRIGITTE'S BATTLE

Take Brigitte Bardot, once Hollywood's biggest sex bomb.

She now lives the life of a recluse, surrounded by the animals she has rescued, in her St Tropez villa La Madrague.

'It was a choice I was perfectly happy with,' she says.

'Since then I have dedicated my life, and a very large part of my wealth, to the protection of animals.

'I prefer the company of animals to that of people because they never disappoint you. Someone once said that man's best friends never hurt us until they die.

'I've had a great love of animals all my life. I can't explain why. I've always felt closer to them than to people. I can't give you a reason for that either. It's just the way it is.'

Brigitte, who has 21 dogs, 20 cats, horses, goats, sheep and a donkey called Mimosa, says she never turns away a stray animal in need.

She has taken in old horses saved from the abattoir and ensured that huntsmen seeking foxes or wild boar know that if they venture onto her land they will be treated as trespassers.

Trappers using legholds now declared illegal in most of Europe have come in for a particularly hard Bardot tongue-lashing.

She has even fronted her own TV series – *Hunting and Hunters* – in which she took on one of the most powerful lobbies in France, the farmers.

Brigitte pointed out that a staggering 73 per cent of French people thought hunters abused their rights. She quoted 66 per cent support for her dream of making them face much tougher rules covering the way they operate.

But her biggest campaign to date is an attempt to have all of France's estimated 35 million stray cats and dogs sterilized, a move she argues would drastically reduce the miseries suffered by strays.

Such is her passion that she has willed her £2 million home to her Bardot Foundation for the Protection of Animals.

The actress, star of *And God Created Woman*, has a pessimistic view of the future.

She speaks of the world getting worse for both people and animals – a phenomenon she calls 'the decline of the end of the millenium'.

She adds: 'Too many people who are in a position to change things are indifferent.

'Existing laws are not implemented. Poachers are devastating wildlife, destroying everything for money. Laboratories use animals in vivisection experiments that are like something out of a science fiction horror film.

'I'm a vegetarian. I only wear clothes made from cotton or wool. I don't buy any cosmetics tested on animals.

'Learning to respect animal life would teach us to respect the lives of the weakest humans, who are suffering in the same intolerable way.'

MODEL ON THE CATWALK

If the prospect of caring for 20 cats is daunting, pity Celia Hammond, one of the most celebrated models ever to stare from the cover of *Vogue*.

She gave up the glamour and glitz of her 1960s career to devote herself to rescuing strays – a full-time job she now describes as 'the most important thing in my life'.

Now she has 250 in the catteries of her home in east Sussex, southern England, with dozens more sick or injured animals

Below: *Actress Brigitte Bardot with some of the stray dogs that have become the focus of her animal welfare campaign.*

allowed to roam the rooms of her house.

Her obsession – she readily admits it is one – started when a photographer friend gave her three kittens, Rosie, Dozy and Sophie.

Gradually she took more and more interest in the welfare of strays, somehow working her rescue missions into the demanding life of a top model.

She says: 'It got to the point where it became more important than my work.

'I was not turning up to jobs and pretending I was ill when really I was out rescuing strays.'

Celia's ultimate goal – like Bardot's in France – is to tackle the root cause of homeless cats and dogs in Britain by equipping spaying clinics capable of operating at very low costs.

In the meantime she does her bit by making night trips to London four times per week to track down and rescue strays.

Most she finds trapped in rundown or derelict buildings or in the dock wastelands east of the City.

'The obsession isn't about being surrounded with cats,' she says.

'To be honest, I'd be quite happy to be with one cat, or even no cats.

'The obsession is to solve the problem of there being two and a half million stray cats and dogs in Britain at the moment. I want to do something about that by preventing them from breeding.'

Celia says she'd love to spend more time on her social life, or indulging her hobby of prowling round auction rooms and antique shops.

But she admits: 'If I did I would torture myself about all the animals that were suffering because I had taken the day off.'

There does seem to be something about cats that inspires almost total devotion from showbusiness types. You'd think ordinary toms and tabbies were hard enough work, yet for some the challenge comes much bigger. Big cats in fact.

THE BIG CATS

Virginia McKenna, known to millions as the star of the tear-jerker *Born Free*, is perhaps the best-known devotee.

During her 11 months filming that classic she and husband Bill Travers found themselves drawn closer and closer into the

lives of the proud beasts working alongside them.

It was an experience which changed her life and made her decide to wage a personal war against conditions captive animals have to endure.

In 1983 an elephant she'd worked with on a movie titled *An Elephant Called Slowly* was given a new home at London Zoo. The animal later sickened and eventually had to be put to sleep.

For Virginia it was a massive emotional blow and she vowed to launch her own charity dedicated to investigate the treatment of caged animals.

Today Zoo Check is one of the most

Above: *Former* Vogue *cover girl Celia Hammond (right) with fellow model Sue Gunn. Celia began taking in cats in the early 1980s – now she has 250.*

Above: *Born free: Virginia McKenna and Bill Travers with their beloved lion, Elsa.*

THE FILM CHANGED HER LIFE AND SHE DECIDED TO FIGHT HER OWN PERSONAL WAR.

---

powerful voices in the entire animal rights lobby.

Virginia says: 'People should only have access to zoos if they don't cause suffering to animals.

'For example, it's totally unacceptable to have polar bears in zoos. They're so deprived by the way they're kept.

'I'm also very against keeping elephants in captivity. In the wild they have a complex life-style that is impossible to duplicate in a zoo or circus.'

She now spends most of her time on the charity's workload after taking a decision not to return to the theatre. She describes her acting career as a 'wonderful innings' but insists animal welfare is now more important.

'Having seen so many animals in zoos in so many countries, and given the terrible images of their plight that I carry about with me always, I know I must do something for them.

'That's what my heart says.

'I know some scientists, the boffins, might say: "She's just a nutty actress."

'I may be a bit nutty but I feel quit rational.'

Another Hollywood star brought to th animal rights cause through films is Tipp Hedren, star of Hitchcock's *The Birds* an mother of Melanie Griffith.

She was shooting (cameras, not guns) i Africa in the late 1960s when she and ex husband Noel Marshall found themselve entranced by lions.

They started their own temporar sanctuary, made the film *Roar* with the 'pets' and then bought a ranch near L Angeles to give the animals a permaner reserve.

Tippi says: 'Many of the animals we very old, and didn't last long.

'We now have great cats which inclu African lions, American mountain lion Bengali and Siberian tigers, black-spott leopards and cougars, two Afric elephants and my pot-bellied pig, S Winston Churchill.

'The great cats have mystique, they' magnificent and they have a frightenir quality about them.

'We try to understand them. We know what makes them happy, what makes them angry. That's very important as they are volatile animals, quite capable of destroying you. One did attack me and had my head in its mouth.

'But they're very special. They accept each other just as they are.'

She describes herself as 'the luckiest lady in the world' to live with such exotic species around her. And, she freely admits, they dictate almost everything she does.

One of the tigers, named Natasha, is so jealous of Tippi's time she will never let her do anything other than offer her full attention.

That means taking a newspaper or magazine out of the actress's hand and, if necessary, tearing it to shreds.

But with big cats around, Tippi is tolerant.

She says: 'People should understand that every single animal, every critter on the Earth has a personality which is magical. They are thinking, feeling beings and they have every right to a dignified life.'

Tippi has ploughed every penny of her savings into her reserve. And with a staff of 15 to pay, it's not a cheap hobby.

'I've probably taken on more than I can handle,' she admits.

'But I still take great joy in hearing the lions roaring.'

ANIMAL WELFARE

Famous names who have the animal welfare 'obsession' recognize that unless they're careful, their own living can be jeopardized.

Loretta Swit – Hot Lips Houlihan in the comedy series M*A*S*H – jokes: 'I can't remember a time when I wasn't interested in animal welfare.

'It's really my second career, though my agent would say: "No, it's her first." '

As tough-talking Major Houlihan Loretta strikes a blow for women's equality with almost every order she blasts out. Off screen, her one-woman campaign for animals is fought with every bit as much intensity.

She says: 'Wildlife is my great love but it's not just a question of loving animals.

'The whole world loves animals. The people who own and love animals also hunt, wear fur coats, eat meat, wear leather, have crocodile belts.

> **THE GREAT CAT RIPPED THE NEWSPAPER FROM THE ACTRESS'S HAND AND TORE IT TO SHREDS.**

Below: *When Tippi Hendren puts the cat out for the night she needs to have her wits about her. Here she and husband Noel Marshall pet one of their Siberian tigers.*

Right: *Loretta Swit with a young seal. 'It's the world I care about,' she says.*

Below: *Loretta with a friendly turtle.*

'I don't do any of these things and actually fight for animals.

'I've got dirt under my nails and been bitten by mosquitos tagging sea turtles and counting their eggs so I could raise money for a beach in Florida where the turtles come every year and lay their eggs. If the land gets developed they will die.'

She is furious with those who say she's 'crazy' about animals.

'That's not it at all. I'm not just an animal lover. It's the world I care about the rainforest and the fact that we lose one species every four hours.'

Loretta supports around 14 separate animal welfare groups, including Beauty Without Cruelty and the US Human Society. She agrees with Bardot and Celi Hammond that one of the great scandals of our modern civilization is the number of strays on the streets.

The figure of five million animals a year put down in the USA horrifies her especially as the country's puppy 'farms keep turning out more and more.

She said: 'We're all animals. Some of run around on two legs, some on four some swim, some fly.

'And this is the only place we all have.

Other big names in the animal right business include Dustin Hoffman, Jac Nicholson, Tom Cruise, Barbra Streisan

Joanna Lumley and Live Aid mastermind Bob Geldof.

Joanna is one of the co-founders of the international Elefriends campaign, set up to persuade consumers not to buy ivory.

She was appalled to discover how the animals are slaughtered by poachers toting Russian-made submachine guns, who then saw off the tusks for sale abroad.

Joanna says: 'People have stopped wearing furs because they now know about the cruelty and damage.

'We want to do the same for elephants. If people know what is involved they will stop buying ivory.

'Elephants live like we do. They are infinitely kind. They are not predators.

'They look after their own.'

But if famous names generally carry clout in the cause of animals, one husband-and-wife team is the undisputed champion.

Ex-Beatle Paul McCartney and his American-born wife Linda are ready to take on all comers in their support for animal rights.

That includes big multi-national companies who have spent years crafting their public image.

One US car maker with a record of conducting animal experiments was banned from taking advertising space on McCartney's 1993 world tour.

McCartney threatened to make his own TV and radio adverts telling the world the nature of the experiments. Jubilant campaigners immediately rang the company telling them: 'McCartney is getting involved.

'Do you really want to take on Paul McCartney?'

The company quickly issued a statement making clear it 'no longer had any animal trauma research activity'.

McCartney, who has sold 38 million records since the Beatles split up, is not one to hold back on his adopted cause.

He and Linda are both vegetarians, sworn to 'never eat anything with a face', and have carried out scores of high-profile campaigns to publicize their beliefs.

On one occasion the couple bought and freed lobsters destined for the dinner table. They have also forced fox hunters off their land, threatening legal action against anybody who defies them.

Paul regularly attacks the barbaric slaughter of whales. 'Keep the sea blue, not red' is one of his favourite slogans.

He also made a personal plea to US President Ronald Reagan to save tiny long-tailed Macaques monkeys from medical experiments. Thirty of them were used, more than half of which died.

On his record 'Looking For Changes' – described as McCartney's most powerful protest song to date – he portrays shocking images of life in a research laboratory.

One line goes: 'I saw a rabbit with its eyes full of tears, the lab that owned her had been doing it for years.'

Another reads: 'I saw a monkey that was learning to choke, a guy beside him gave him cigarettes to smoke.'

The McCartneys have been vegetarian since 1973, when Linda and Paul sat down to a leg of roast lamb … and then noticed some live ones gambolling about in a field outside.

Linda is now trying to re-educate the palates of the Western world with her own

Above: *Paul McCartney is a leading voice in animal rights campaigning. Major companies with a questionable record of experimentation on captive creatures think twice before taking him on.*

Above: *Carla Lane at home. 'Animals have pure and innocent souls and humans haven't,' she says.*

brand of meatless meals. She's made a good start, with 50 million of the meals sold.

She says: 'I'm desperate about vegetarianism. We're all talking about a peaceful world and yet you can legally take a cow, a pig, a sheep and murder it.

'Now I think animals should have a little more dignity. I just don't believe in the word "slaughterhouse".

'It's an evil thing, like I think Hitler was an evil man, but we moved the people out and the chickens in.

'I just try and plant a seed. I do kiss people who eat meat. I have a lot of friends and relatives who eat meat and they're lovely people.'

Her tactics are to combine high-profile stunts – such as her letter to Australian prime minister and pig farmer Paul Keating – and the art of gentle persuasion, namely her vegetarian cookbook.

Of Keating Linda says: 'He's a pig farmer and I believe if you're going to lead a country you have to be a great person.

'So I sent him and his wife my cookbook and just mentioned that they might think and grow, that there might be a better way. I've probably bristled him, I'm sure they think "how dare she, more money than sense".'

The cookbook, she insists, isn't for vegetarians. It's to help convert long-standing meat eaters.

'I did it to say to the truck driver "You can eat great, I can make it easy for your wife".

'You can make a stew out of a vegg

burger, no gristle, no pain, no death, no fat.

'People ask where I get my strength if I don't eat flesh. I say, where do the elephant, the gorilla, the bull get their strength?

'They don't eat meat.'

One of Linda and Paul's closest allies is British playwright Carla Lane, author of hit TV comedies such as *The Liver Birds*, *Butterflies*, *Bread* and *Luv*.

She has carved out a hugely successful and lucrative career. Yet she has sworn to leave every penny of her wealth to the creatures she cares for at her £1.5 million sanctuary in the heart of the Sussex countryside.

That's good news for the likes of a one-winged heron, 800 birds, a blind hamster, a limping pheasant, 20 goats, 10 dogs, 15 cats and a field full of mud-caked ponies.

Carla, who runs the Animal Line organization – a telephone helpline for anyone looking after sick creatures – with Linda McCartney says: 'People might think I'm crazy.

'But animals have pure and innocent souls, and humans haven't.

'I have talked to my sons, Carl and Nigel, and told them that neither they nor their children will get any money – it will all go on the sanctuary.

'But they said "Mum, if that's what you're happy doing, it's fine with us." '

Carla's attempt to find havens for her animal friends extends to a tiny island off the north-west coast of Wales. She bought it in 1991 after hearing that the wildlife which lived there was dying.

She says: 'I went to see it two weeks after I bought it.

'All the animals had died. Others swam away. But one little deer swam back and gave birth on the island.

'When the baby was 4 months old we took it back to the mainland. We did the same the following year. And now there is a little herd of deer running amok somewhere around Abersoch.

'On the island itself we've got lots of little black rabbits which originated in the 12th century there. And we've got every bird you can possibly think of, and lots of lovely wild flowers.

'I've got a little croft on the island, but I never stay there because it's very steep and I'm very frightened of heights. I'm also frightened of water.

'How I came to buy an island I'll never know.'

'KEEP THE SEA BLUE, NOT RED.'

Below: *Linda McCartney and Carla. Their Animal Line organization is aimed at giving practical advice to anyone caring for sick creatures.*

The British Homing World's
PIGEON RACING
GAZETTE

NOVEMBER 1993

No. 11. Vol 49.

Price £1.20p

Peter Bennett

"Hillside Vend"

First Open N...

BIRDS OF A FEATHER

Birds of all feathers have captivated the human race for centuries with their lovely songs, their brilliant plumage and their fantastic powers of flight, but at times the relationship between people and their birds has had a deeper significance ...

In countryside and cities, on mountain ranges and throughout suburban towns, you never have to look far to 'watch the birdie'. The sound of a warbling song and the sight of a small feathered bundle hopping about without a care is one of the wonders of nature that each of us can enjoy, no matter where we live. And from the soaring flight of the magnificent eagle to the tiny, fluttering lark, birds have been a source of fascination for people throughout the centuries.

Legend has it that Icarus lost his life in his bid to mimic the flight of a bird, and no aircraft has yet managed to master the graceful skyward movements and aerobatic skills displayed by our feathered friends.

Even now these captivating creatures are the centre of interest for many, and that interest can sometimes border on obsession.

PIGEON POST

To the untrained eye pigeons may seem to proliferate in our capitals. To many they are simply a nuisance, but an expert will soon spot the aristocrat of the breed, a racer.

The world's most valuable pigeon cost £110,000 in 1992. British breeder Michael Massarella parted with the cash for Invincible Spirit, a pigeon who earned his colours by beating 27,000 other birds in the Barcelona International, one of the prestige races on the pigeon fanciers' calendar. He completed the 719-mile course in a mere 21 hours.

When it came to getting the bird from its base in Holland, however, the new owner decided against nature's way and in favour of new technology. Luxuriating in a first class seat, the pigeon was served a breakfast of maize, lettuce and mineral water in his posh travelling box.

After touchdown at Gatwick airport he was ferried by chauffeur-driven Rolls-Royce to his new home at Louella Pigeon World near Loughborough, Leicestershire, for a new life as a super stud.

For Mr Massarella there were no qualms about parting with the vast sum for a pigeon. At the time he said: 'We are absolutely delighted with him. We hope he will have many happy and productive years with us.'

It is not the first time he has shelled out big money for a cooing wonder. In 1988 he paid £77,000 for Champion Smaragd, then the world's most pricey pigeon. Pigeons like these can achieve breathtaking speeds. In 1914 a racing pigeon travelling over an 80-mile course in Northern Ireland flew at 93.55 mph.

But pigeon racing isn't only about skill

Above: *Icarus tumbles from heaven after his wax wings are melted by the Sun. For thousands of years man has been captivated by the secret of flight.*

Opposite: *The* **Pigeon Racing Gazette** – *the pigeon fancier's Bible. Sums of up to £110,000 are paid for the right bird.*

and speed. As with all things, luck plays its part. Scratch the wonder pigeon found that out.

He was one of 3,500 birds who set off on a race from the heart of France to their base in Britain, some 700 miles away. A cloak of thick fog over the English Channel together with some unseasonal storms sent the birds' homing mechanisms haywire and most of them ended up in Belgium. Scratch was the only bird to make it home to Yorkshire in time.

His astonishing success won him all 25 prizes which had been up for grabs – two trophies and a total of £600.

Above: *The Roman emperor Honorius was among the earliest pigeon fanciers.*

Right: *Not all pigeon lofts are wood shacks. This architectural masterpiece is in Cappadocia, Turkey.*

'I knew Scratch was good,' commented owner Alan Embleton, aged 15. 'But I never expected him to do this well.'

Eventually 29 other birds turned up but they were too late to be considered for the competition, held in July 1992.

Yorkshire pigeon official Peter Kerr was baffled. 'Thousands of pounds worth of prize-winning birds have disappeared off the face of the Earth.'

Sadly it is never easy for racing pigeons, who not only have extreme weather conditions to contend with but also high-sided lorries, birds of prey – and the neighbourhood moggies.

Fate dealt a cruel blow to prize pigeon Percy in the same month. Still puffing after finishing a race from France he was crunched by a cat called Sylvester. Dismayed owner Pat Lees, aged 55, said: 'I'd been waiting hours for him to turn up when this fat cat jumped out and grabbed him in its teeth.'

It took an hour and a half to snatch poor Percy from the jaws of the ginger tom, by which time he had died. But there was enough time to clock him in and win a posthumous third prize in the race.

When pigeon fancier Ken Warkup found a cat dining out on one of his prize birds he decided to take revenge. Unfortunately not only did the cat scupper one of his birds, it also landed him in court.

Enraged Ken stuffed the cat called Sam in a sack and dumped him in a field 12 miles away from home in Bridlington, Yorkshire. However, the cat was not to be outdone and found his own way home five months later looking rather sorry for himself. When Ken was quizzed by an officer from the Royal Society for the Prevention of Cruelty to Animals, he confessed.

THE PIGEON SURVIVED THE
PERILOUS JOURNEY — ONLY
TO DIE A LINGERING DEATH
IN THE JAWS OF THE
NEIGHBOURHOOD MOGGIE.

Left: *This woodcut of 1523 shows men of a besieged city summoning help with carrier pigeons.*

Below: *A carrier pigeon with message case attached to its leg. The birds have even ferried ransom demands.*

In March 1992 he told magistrates: 'I've bred pigeons for 24 years and some of them are worth a lot of money. I don't want them ending up as cat meat.' After admitting a cruelty charge he was given a 12-month conditional discharge.

With their amazing ability to find a way home, it is not surprising that an enterprising villain seized on pigeon post as a way to cash in on crime. Taiwan police were left in a flap when the owners of stolen cars were told to cough up for the return of their missing motor.

The hapless victims were directed to a local park to find a bamboo bird cage and instructed to attach the ransom money in a pouch to the neck of the pigeon inside. When the bird was released, there was little the surveillance team could do other than watch helplessly through binoculars as the pigeon made a dash for home, soon lost from sight among buildings and trees.

It seems likely the person profiting from his pigeons was an armchair crook who didn't even bother to steal the car in the

Top: *'Cher Ami' – saviour of US troops.*

Above: *GI Joe with the Dickin Medal.*

THE PLUCKY BIRD TOOK TO THE AIR AGAIN, DESPITE FOUR BULLET WOUNDS; THE SOLDIERS' LIVES DEPENDED ON HIM REACHING HIS DESTINATION.

first place. He simply seized on the names and numbers of genuine victims from the local newspapers. Police were convinced he was pulling off a hoax because none of the vehicles turned up despite the payments made by the owners.

Smart as he or she may have been, however, the money made out of the scam was only corn. The bird was unable to carry large amounts of cash because it would have been hampered by the weight.

Of course, it is not just in the present that people have discovered the uses of pigeons. Among the earliest domesticated birds, they were held sacred as long ago as 4500 BC in Mesopotamia and they were used to carry the results in the original Olympic Games to outlying villages. In 1150 the first pigeon post was set up by the sultan of Baghdad.

Initally brought to Britain by the Crusaders, pigeons were once the reserve of royalty, nobility and the clergy, and until two centuries ago usually ended up on the menu.

Then their uses, particularly in times of conflict, became clear.

The most famed homing bird of World War 1 was a cock named Cher Ami who was given the Croix de Guerre, a top French military honour. One of 500,000 birds brought to war-torn France by the American Expeditionary Force, he served with the infantry. On 4 October 1918, his battalion was being shelled by not only enemy German guns but also American positions, in error.

With defeat and annihilation in prospect, the pigeon was sent back to base bearing the message: 'Our own artillery is dropping a barrage directly on us ... for heaven's sake stop it.'

But Cher Ami was unable to dodge the enemy fire. He was felled almost instantly by a bullet and plunged to the ground. In despair, an American yelled: 'Cher Ami, go home.' With that the plucky pigeon once again took to the air, suffered three more bullet wounds which destroyed his breast bone, right leg and one of his eyes, and flew an incredible 24 miles in 25 minutes to the division headquarters. The battalion was saved, thanks to this doughty winged messenger, who was taken back home to the US and survived until June 1919. After his death he was stuffed and put on display in Washington's Smithsonian Institute.

During World War 2 no fewer than 31 birds were awarded the Dickin Medal for bravery.

One of them, Mary, survived an attack by a hawk, enemy fire, a 1000 lb bomb which exploded outside her loft in Exeter and later, a gash which ran the length of her body. Still she refused to give up the fight for life and for her country.

Another, GI Joe, an American pigeon, carried a swift message to Air Command when they were about to bomb an enemy position telling them that their target had been taken by the Allies. A few moments later and countless soldiers would have been slaughtered by their own comrades.

The multi-talented pigeon has also been found to be an excellent quality inspector, turfing out plastic nuts and other components with defects in a British car factory production line, all for the reward of some grain. A Russian scientist discovered pigeons could classify up to 4,000 ball bearings an hour.

ROYAL RAVENS

The British royal family's interests lie not so much in pigeons but in ravens. Folklore says the Crown and Empire will fall if the sleek black ravens which make their home at the Tower of London disappear.

Just to be on the safe side, the rave

population which freely roams the grounds of the Tower by day has clipped wings to be sure they don't flee under cover of darkness. They are so tame they are whistled into bed by the Beefeaters.

Although the species has bred successfully in London for centuries, it is rare for the birds at the Tower to hatch eggs, probably because the mating ritual involves some airborne antics. Many there today were brought from sanctuaries as orphans from nests elsewhere. So it was with some excitement that fledglings were welcomed at the Tower in 1989, the first to be born there in 300 years.

A nesting box well away from the gaze of gawping tourists had been provided and five eggs duly appeared, thanks to Charlie and Rhys, two of eight birds permanently on the site. Due to overcrowding, the young ones were taken off to sanctuaries around the country, still the property of the queen and liable to be summoned at a moment's notice if duty calls.

A deputy governor, Colonel John Wynn, explains: 'Charles II wanted to get rid of hundreds that were around during his reign.

Left: *Charles II. He was advised against wiping out the hundreds of ravens in London. Was this the origin of the Tower legend?*

It is said that he was advised to keep some of the birds. The legend that the Crown and Empire will fall if the Tower loses its ravens may date from this incident.

'They are enormously popular with our visitors, particularly the children. Among the attractions, they come behind the Crown

Below: *A raven at the Tower of London. If the birds leave, according to legend, the monarchy will fall.*

THE JUDGE ORDERED THE ROWDY ROOSTER TO KEEP ITS BEAK SHUT UNTIL BREAKFAST TIME.

Jewels and equal with the instruments of torture, which is pretty high up.'

HENPECKED

When it comes to pets it is more likely that hens or ducks will rule the roost. Sometimes the bond between people and their feathered friends gets to be no yolk, as Cathy Brooks discovered. For Cathy, aged 28, isn't the only woman in her husband's life. She must vie for his affections with a hand-reared hen called Kiki and is one of Britain's few hen-pecked wives.

Husband Keith, aged 47, is so attached to the 7-year-old white hen Kiki that he lets her live a life of luxury in their three-bedroomed home in Canterbury, Kent, where she spends the night in her own chair in the kitchen and joins the family for meals at the dinner table.

Cathy says: 'Kiki was on the scene before I came along and Keith is very attached to her. He says she's almost human. I think she's just a bird that makes a mess on the carpet and goes for

your dinner when you are eating.'

Keith hatched out Kiki in an incubator. 'There was an immediate parental bonding and now she's absolutely one of the family.'

Kiki might be a bird with plenty of personality but she is a mere shadow of some of her bigger cousins bred in the USA. The largest chicken ever recorded was a 22 lb rooster called Weirdo in California. Born as a result of cross-breeding, he was also unusually aggressive and killed two cats, crippled a dog and ripped through a wire fence to maul another giant rooster. There was certainly no doubt cast on his sexuality.

But there have been cases of chickens changing sex and even cockerels laying eggs. The sex change is the result of a hormone imbalance which might rectify itself given time. To the disbelief of experts worldwide, Sri Lankan housewife Swarna Kulasiri reported that her lone cock in a 100-strong poultry run had begun to lay an egg a day. So perplexed was she by the amazing feat, she isolated the bird, which

Below: *Britain's most vocal cockerel, Corky, with his original owner Margery Johns. He would wake up at 3.30 am.*

retained its large comb and cock-a-doodle-do crow, and watched with her own eyes as he produced a large, brown egg.

While they may be able to switch sex, there seems little a cockerel can do about its morning call. British justice said differently when it pronounced a cockerel must keep its beak shut until breakfast time because of the disturbance he caused to neighbours.

Corky, the early riser, was the bird at the heart of a neighbourhood dispute which was eventually waged in court.

His owner, Margery Johns, of Hartland, North Devon, was fond of the 4-year-old rowdy rooster who serviced 14 hens at her home. But neighbour John Ritchings and his wife Lindsey were plagued by Corky's crowing, which they claimed began as early as 3.30 am. Former personnel director Mr Ritchings started keeping data on the cock-a-doodle-doos on his computer.

First he had a relocation order slapped on Corky, which had the bird ousted from his henhouse to a distant greenhouse. Then, when a noise prosecution against Mrs Johns and her bird brought by the local council failed, Mr Ritchings sought another court order, this time to stop Corky from disturbing the peace.

At Taunton County Court in March 1993, Mr Ritchings explained: 'The cock would wake us as early as 3.30 in the morning, most of the time with a quick burst. There would then be a peaceable period, another quick burst, another peaceful period and then at 5 or 7 am the crowing became almost continuous and it became very difficult to get any sleep.

'When nothing was done about the problem I began making a computerized database in which I made notes of the exact minute of Corky's crows and the effect it had on my sleep pattern.'

Above: *Yagamo, 'the arrowed duck'. He became a huge crowd puller in Tokyo until he was captured in early 1993 to have the arrow removed. Vets found the plucky bird had also been wounded by shotgun pellets.*

THE ANGLERS WERE HOPING FOR A NIBBLE – BUT ALL THEY GOT WAS A NASTY PECK.

Noise pollution inspector Christopher Utting agreed the crowing was too loud after becoming an early bird himself to measure the nuisance. But other villagers who had never complained about the fowl noise thought differently, believing townies were trying to remould the centuries-old traditions of the rural areas. A coachload travelled 60 miles to support Mrs Johns and Corky, claiming she had every right to keep farm animals in the countryside with all their attendant noises.

Judge Malcolm Cotterill didn't agree, however. He made a gagging order against Corky between the hours of midnight and 7 am. Mrs Johns – who said she might as well try to stop the traffic noise as prevent Corky from doing what came naturally – even tried soundproofing her henhouse. All to no avail. She was landed with costs amounting to some £20,000.

Judge Cotterill then made an appeal for calm in the tiny village. 'I regret the fact this case has been elevated to a crusade on behalf of oppressed chickens,' he announced.

Afterwards, Mrs Johns said: 'I feel there is an important principle involved. Country life is country life and to complain about a cockerel crowing is the thin end of the wedge.

'A mile away from us there is a farmer whose cows are being monitored for the noise they make. They're talking about smells now. They want to deodorize farmyards. Well, I would much rather smell cow muck than a London bus but you don't get country bumpkins moving to London and demanding that they stop the buses, do you?'

Corky was saved from exile by the offer of a new home from a farm-turned-tourist attraction in the vicinity where he could crow at all hours.

LUCKY DUCKS

Ducks, somewhat quieter creatures altogether, have also earned a special place in people's hearts, none more so than Donald, the lady duck mascot of the 2nd Gordon Highlanders who was captured during active service in World War 2 and held in a Japanese prisoner of war camp in Thailand. Usually all animals belonging to prisoners were destroyed, but duck master

Corporal William Gray told the guards that Donald was a sacred bird, worshipped every morning by the company, as was common practice between men and ducks throughout their native Scotland.

By way of reward Donald during 18 months in captivity laid 163 eggs which were dished up to ailing internees. She returned to Scotland with Corporal Gray and spent the rest of her days in Forgue, Aberdeenshire.

The longest living ducks on record were a pair owned by Gladys Blackbeard of Cape Province, South Africa. Given to her by a soldier in 1917, they lived to celebrate their 49th birthday in June 1966. Ducks are normally dead at half that grand old age.

Perhaps the luckiest duck of all was Yagamo of Japan. The pintail duck was shot through the middle with a bow but survived even though the 30 cm pink carbon-fibre arrow which impaled his back protruded from his stomach. He walked and flew with ease and there was no sign of blood.

First spotted in January 1993, he was soon the centre of attraction for crowds of concerned on-lookers and a host of TV cameras and reporters. Yagamo – which means 'the arrowed duck' – wasn't struck on being a star.

He tried to elude the throngs by flying between ponds in the capital, Tokyo, until pleas for peace from zoo officials trying to catch the duck in order to remove the arrow had some effect. On 12 February he was netted and taken to Ueno Zoo where the arrow was taken out. X-rays revealed the bird also had two shotgun pellets lodged in its body but surgeons decided to leave them because of the danger of a prolonged operation. Eleven days after the operation Yagamo was released into the wild once more, ready to join the annual spring migration to Siberia.

RARE BIRDS

Canary Jimmy was not so lucky and succumbed to death back in 1920, but his owner, cobbler Edidio Rusomanno fulfilled a promise to give his much loved pet a fabulous send-off. Jimmy's body was put in a fine white casket and carried by hearse followed by two coaches and 15-piece band to its final resting place in local New Jersey park. Edidio wept in front of the 10,000 people who turned up for the event before returning to a slap-up feast at his shop.

Another pet bird, the budgerigar, has won the affection of dedicated owners everywhere, thanks to its curious ability to mimic language. Budgies originated in Australia but came to Britain back in 1840 with returning naturalist John Gould. Now there are probably more caged budgies than there are wild ones.

One of the world's longest surviving budgies was a hen called Charlie who died at her London home in June 1977 after living for more than 29 years. One of the strangest was Jenny, a budgie owned by June Lowton, of Nottingham, who refused to roost on her perch like others of her kind but snoozed flat out on the bottom of the cage with her feet stuck in the air, looking much as a dead budgie would.

Willy, a fly-by-night budgie, was the subject of one of the greatest fishermen's tales ever told. Three anglers spent hours waiting for a nibble as they bobbed about in the English Channel in the summer of 1991. In fact, they ended up getting a nasty peck.

Just as it seemed they were going to return home empty handed they caught – a budgie. The worn-out bird flopped down in the sea beside their boat and was netted by

Below: *Goldie the golden eagle. After his escape from Regent's Park Zoo in 1965 he stayed on the run for two weeks. He survived on food scraps and the odd juicy London duck!*

THE MIGHTY OWL
TERRORIZED LOCAL
RESIDENTS AND EVEN
DIVEBOMBED A
ROTTWEILER.

Below: *Ostriches can deliver a kick capable of killing ... they are also no mean soccer players.*

the three men, their only catch of the trip. He rewarded them for the free ride to terra firma with a series of sharp nips.

One of the men, Geoff Lowley, said: 'Our wives were expecting some nice plaice or skate for supper but they thought it was hilarious when all we came back with was a budgie.'

It's thought the bird escaped from a passing ship. Geoff adopted the little scrap, took him to his home in Torbay, Devon, and christened him Willy. Sadly, a photographer who came to snap the by-now famous flying catch propped open the door of the cage – and Willy proved he was the bird they could not tame by flying off

into the sunset, never to be seen again.

A barred warbler caused just as much of a surprise when it turned up in Britain one December day. The ornithological rarity touched down in South Woodham Ferrers, Essex, in 1992 when it should, in fact, have been in Kenya escaping the winter chill of its East European home. Soon, avid bird-watchers – or twitchers as they are known – from all over the country gathered at the spot, but the warbler's first days in frosty Britain were also to be its last.

Local birdwatcher Ray Trevett explained: 'The county bird recorder came down and confirmed the sighting. Soon there were about 25 people here with cameras and binoculars. It was all fluffed up and survived two nights of heavy frost. It was hopping around happily.

'This large black cat had been patrolling around. Suddenly we noticed the bird wasn't in its tree. The cat appeared with the bird in its mouth. It scampered off and by the time we found the bird it had been decapitated.

'When I broke the news to the birdwatchers they were very upset. It was a major twitch.'

Another rare sight in British skies is the golden eagle. Once familiar over the country's mountain ranges, this magnificent bird of prey was blamed by farmers for early lamb deaths and was hunted, poisoned or trapped until numbers plummeted to crisis point. Only a carefully planned programme ensured its survival.

But residents of London who never would have dreamed an eagle would be swooping in the capital's skies had an unexpected treat in March 1965 when Goldie the golden eagle fled from his home in Regent's Park Zoo.

Crowds turned out to see the tawny hawk-like bird, some 3 ft tall, perched in tree tops above the park, causing traffic chaos. Goldie, meanwhile, was revelling in his newfound freedom, stretching his wings at will after being penned in for most of his seven years.

When keepers were unable to tempt him back, they confessed he could survive for years in the park, picking off ducks from the pond when he was hungry. Mostly people were delighted he had escaped from the confines of the cage where he had been kept in captivity. In fact, he was recaptured after a fortnight, only to make a second bid for freedom some nine months later.

Thor, the European eagle owl, also caused a stir, this time in Nottingham in 1991 when he bowled over a man in the street. Thor fled his aviary home in Derbyshire when it was damaged in a storm.

The 2 ft tall bird with a wing span of 4 ft flattened woodyard worker Michael Barke, aged 23, as he made his way to work. Afterwards Mr Barke said: 'I was walking down the road when it came out of nowhere – it just went for me and headbutted me, I'm still shaking.'

During his brief spell of freedom before recapture, Thor alarmed local residents by peering in their windows at night. The mighty owl, the world's largest species, also divebombed a hefty Rottweiler dog.

The largest known bird in the world is the ostrich, which can reach 8 ft in height and weigh up to 300 lb. At a canter, the flightless bird can reach 30 mph and will deliver a hefty kick by way of attack. So imagine the surprise of brothers Nathan and Daniel Pedley when just such a bird joined in their game of football in the leafy and suburban environs of Stokenchurch, Buckinghamshire, in November 1989. The runaway bird – a rhea, which looks like an ostrich – niftily side-stepped the soccer-mad boys and pursuing police with some impressive dribbling skills. 'Unfortunately it was flattened later in a tackle by a car on the M40,' commented a police spokesman.

But mystery surrounds the allegation that a possibly larger breed, thought to be extinct, is actually surviving in New Zealand. Biologists thought that lanky moas died out at least 400 years ago.

Yet in January 1993 hotel owner and hiker Paddy Freaney and two companions saw a 6 ft tall bird with reddish-brown and grey feathers almost to its knees, a long neck and large feet hiding in a bush. As the creature fled across a stream, Freaney fired off a shot on his camera and also took photos of what he claimed were footprints.

At first the country's Department of Conservation was intrigued by the claims and the inconclusive photograph and considered a probe. But claims that Freaney was a publicity-seeking hoaxer persuaded them to ditch their plans. There

were allegations and counter-allegations about the authenticity of the photos and the witnesses. Even news that two German tourists had seen what they believed to be moas in the same region eight months prior to the incident failed to convince the authorities.

In fact, there have been alleged sightings of the distinctive bird throughout New Zealand's South Island during the past 100 years. Freaney responded to the government's lack of interest by launching his own investigation. It looks as if it is another enduring mystery of Yeti-sized proportions for humanity to ponder.

Above: *Goldie the golden eagle arrives safely back in the arms of his keeper. Yet just two weeks later he made another bid for freedom.*

SHAGGY DOG STORIES

Since the first dog came in from the wild night, tempted by the warmth of the campfire and the smell of roasting meat, the dog's loyalty, love and bravery has proved time and time again that he is indeed man's very best friend.

They're both hunter and bodyguard, sometimes lifesavers … and always friends to the end.

Since their prehistoric ancestors *Tomarctus* first roamed the Earth some 15 million years ago, dogs have emerged as one of our most successful species.

That's partly because they carved out an early understanding with the dominant animal – man – so ensuring that while other beasts got left out in the cold, they had the chance of a bit of fire and a few scraps of meat.

In return those first 'pampered' pooches offered a whole range of services for their keep. The most basic was to give warning of an intruder's approach but their intelligence and obedience later marked them out as superb trackers and farm hands.

The relationship has developed to become unique in the animal kingdom. In terms of sheer devotion, bravery and love, no two other species come closer.

FAITHFUL FRIENDS

Take the Scottish terrier Greyfriars Bobby. In the mid-18th century he was the ever-present partner of a Midlothian landowner by the name of Gray and every market day they would stroll into Edinburgh to buy feed and pick up the weekly shopping.

Then, suddenly, Mr Gray was taken ill and died during one of the journeys. He was later buried in the nearby Greyfriars cemetery. In all the drama the fate of poor Bobby went unnoticed.

The morning after the funeral Bobby was found sitting on his master's grave. The churchwarden at first chased him away but after he persistently refused to leave his post, and when the rain and chilly weather left the lonely animal shivering, the warden took pity and tried to feed him.

Bobby quickly made it clear that sweet buns were the only food he fancied, and as word spread among the locals of his extraordinary loyalty he found there was never any shortage of snacks.

Some people tried to adopt him, but he never would stay, always preferring the grave of the only man he loved. So the people clubbed together to build him a small kennel there. Such was his celebrity status that the lord provost of Edinburgh presented him with his own collar, inscribed 'Greyfriars Bobby'.

Opposite: *Greyfriars Bobby.*

Below: *The world's first scuba-diving dog, Mutley, with his American owner Gene Alba. Mutley also liked skiing and motorbike rides.*

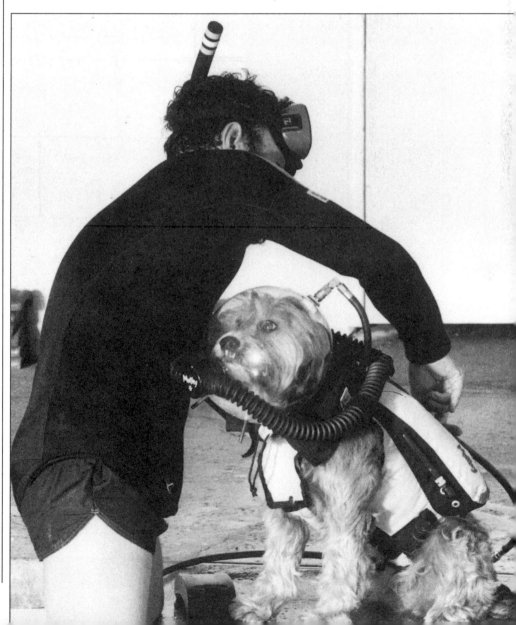

THE FAITHFUL FIDO NEVER GAVE UP HOPE THAT ONE DAY THE MASTER HE LONGED TO SEE WOULD RETURN.

Bobby at last joined his old master in 1872 and of course there could be no argument about where he should be buried. He even had a statue erected on the streets he'd known so well.

Amazingly, such devotion is not particularly unusual. During the war a little Italian mongrel called Fido was left desolate when his master died in a bombing raid in Florence. The pair of them had lived in a village just outside the town and every evening at the same time it was Fido's habit to trot down and meet the bus.

Even when it was clear to everyone else that the dog's master had died, Fido never gave up hope. For an incredible 15 years he continued to lope down to the bus stop to check the faces of the returning commuters in case he recognized the one he longed to see.

In 1958 the villagers of Borgo San Lorenzo put up a memorial to their favourite mongrel and decided the mayor should give him a specially struck gold medal. But just as the beaming burgher prepared to hang it round Fido's neck, the dog raced off.

For a few moments there was alarm and puzzlement among the crowd. Had they scared the little dog? Why was he so desperate to run away? Then someone checked a watch and realized the obvious.

It was time for the bus.

Japan has a similar story of a dog called Hachiko who would walk with his owner to the railway station every day. But one evening his master, a lecturer at Tokyo University, died of a heart attack at work.

Hachiko may have pined, but he never gave up hope. Every day until his death in 1935 he went to the station at his usual time to meet the incoming train.

By then he was almost a national hero, with schools across the nation receiving mini-replicas of him. His face even adorned a postage stamp.

PUPPY-LOVE

The love-bond is something bitches with pups know all about. One of the saddest stories illustrating this is told in Northern Ireland where a retriever gave birth to an unwanted litter. The owner destroyed them

Below: Rally, the radio-controlled police dog, was trained from the age of 3 months to recognize commands over a walkie-talkie. Japanese police use him on mountain rescue work.

Above: *Eyes for the blind; guide dog training is one of the most effective ways to help blind people lead a normal life. Gentle Labradors are the perfect breed.*

at birth, put them in a weighted sack and drove to a lake some 15 miles away, where he hurled the lifeless bodies into the middle.

The bitch was not allowed out of the house for two weeks but on the day the door was opened for her she dashed off and vanished. The man tracked her down 48 hours later to the same lake, where she was swimming around the spot where her puppies lay. She was close to death herself – physically drained by the effort of constant swimming – and her owner was so appalled at what he'd put her through that he vowed he would never again put down another puppy.

There are happier accounts of mother-love in dogs, however. In the spring of 1977 a mongrel called Beauty and her pup found themselves trapped after exploring a deserted house in Worcestershire, central England. For three days the two dogs were left without any food or water and Beauty finally made the decision it was down to her to save herself and her puppy.

Incredibly she squeezed into the bottom of a 45 ft chimney and slowly and painfully wriggled her way up to the top, where she emerged barking loudly enough to bring passers-by running.

On seeing the soot-covered dog it was clear she was raising the alarm and emergency services were called to break into the house. Beauty and her pup were reunited, much to the joy of themselves and their owners. They had apparently begun their adventure after squeezing through a hole in their fence at home.

If Beauty's feat was remarkable, the rescue performed by one bitch with new-born pups was nothing short of a miracle of nature. According to a story in the former *Bath Journal* her heartless owner decided the runt of her four pups should be destroyed. The pitiful animal was hurled into a bucket of water and held down with a mop for a few minutes. The body was then chucked into the ashes box of a fire.

The following morning a dumbstruck servant discovered the bitch still had four, very much alive, puppies. At first he thought another had simply arrived late ... then he checked the ashes box and discovered the dead pup's body was missing.

Incredibly its mum had scrabbled through the cinders and placed the little one back with its brothers and sisters. Milk, warmth and love had done the rest.

> **GASSED, SHOT AND BATTERED, THE DOG COWERED IN THE SHED, TOO TERRIFIED TO EVEN WHIMPER.**

HOUNDED

It's hard to believe man's best friend gets treated in this way and when cases of cruelty hit the headlines the public's outrage knows no bounds. If the guilty parties are featured in the press they can usually rest assured that whatever they did to a dog, around ten million dog lovers are queuing up to do it to them.

The classic example of such sentiments happened in July 1973 when a lovable young beagle cross named Dumpy was unfortunate enough to be seen by the local dog catcher roaming the streets of Salem, Ohio. He was grabbed and bundled into the back of the man's van to be gassed en route to the nearest rubbish tip.

On arrival the catcher threw Dumpy's lifeless body in front of the nearest bulldozer. But to his astonishment the tough little critter began hauling himself out of the sodden trench to escape the huge vehicle bearing down on him.

Immediately the dog catcher squeezed off four bullets, hitting the beagle once in the leg and chest. It wasn't enough to stop Dumpy, who somehow drew on enough strength to keep going.

By now the bulldozer operator, a man called James Gilbert, had halted and leaped down from his cab intent on stopping what he saw as outrageous cruelty. He pleaded with the warden to go after the dog and put him out of his misery but the man refused point-blank. He said he might get his clean boots dirty and Gilbert shouldn't worry – the animal was at death's door anyway.

Gilbert was so traumatized by what he'd witnessed that he ran to telephone a couple of friends, asking them if they could find the dog and ensure it didn't suffer. Jean Fluharty and Joyce Guiler answered the call and in the teeming rain began searching for Dumpy by torchlight. They at last found him sheltering in a shed, too terrified even to whimper.

Later Jean said: 'Every hair on that dog was on end. He was scared to death after all that had happened to him … his eyes were glazed … and he was nothing but mud and blood. He didn't try to bite us, he just didn't make a sound.'

The women took Dumpy – their choice of name – to a local vet who was astounded the animal was still breathing. He patched him up as best he could and amazingly the gallant dog made a full recovery.

Within days of the story getting out hundreds of requests had been fired off from the folk of Salem to give Dumpy a good, caring home. And that's exactly what he got, along with larger than usual amounts of comforting and spoiling.

But what of the dog catcher? Like all the best stories in life, this one ends on a note of justice.

His municipal employers suspended him pending an investigation. This, however, was not enough for the dog lovers of Salem. They began sending threatening letters advising that if they got hold of the man he could expect similar treatment to that Dumpy received. Police had no doubt the threats were serious and the hapless warden was given police protection and advised to be careful in all his movements.

Clearly his life in Salem was untenable. Within months he decided his job wasn't worth the candle and he packed his bags to begin a new life well out of town.

It was, as they say, the right result. And Dumpy remains one of the few hounds in history ever to have driven a dog warden out of business.

DOG-GONE!

Surviving against the odds was also a speciality of a long-haired dachshund called Maxi. He managed to keep himself going for six tortuous weeks in the world's driest place – Chile's Atacama Desert.

In 1977 he visited the area with his owner, a German press attaché called Raban von Mentzingen, who was touring the El Salvador copper mine with his wife and children. The mine was in the heart of the desert and among the country's wildest places.

The Von Mentzingens were paying a final sightseeing visit before their transfer back to Bonn and when Maxi strayed they couldn't wait for him to be found. So local police were given instructions to keep an eye out for him in the hope he could be reunited with the family later.

After a month, all hope faded. Police assured Mr von Mentzingen, by now back in Germany, that his pet could not have survived without food or water in temperatures which could fry bacon in the day and drop below freezing at night.

Then, in March of that year, a Chilean mineral prospector saw the unlikely sight of a long-haired dachshund half-crawling along a sun-parched hillside track 48 miles from the El Salvador mine. Maxi was rescued, flown to Santiago for veterinary treatment and from there was sent on to Germany for a rapturous welcome from his family.

To this day, no one has ever explained how a domestic animal with no experience of hunting (and indeed hardly any food to hunt) managed to survive.

Other fantastic feats to match Maxi's include that of a mongrel called Cindy from San Leandro, California. She was in her owner's car when it was stolen from Stateline, Nevada, on 28 September 1972. Owners Mr and Mrs Ernest Nechvatal sadly gave their pet up for lost. Yet in fact the thieves seem to have returned their car – with Cindy in it – to exactly the same spot after only a few days.

The poor animal was only discovered much later after snowploughs moved in to clear away heavy falls in the area. A workmen found Cindy looking painfully thin, but still alive, on the seat. Her usual weight of 30 lb had been cut by almost half but she had given herself a chance by licking snow that dropped through the slightly open window of the car.

Vets estimated that she had gone without food for up to 73 days.

On a similar note, spare a thought for an Italian wire-haired pointer called Reno. He was trapped under the rubble left by an earthquake in the south of the country for 43 days, finally getting rescued when his owner returned to her devastated home to hear him barking. He had kept alive by drinking rainwater.

A couple of Welsh Jack Russells went through similar ordeals. The first, Judy, spent 36 days trapped down a deep rabbit hole in Builth Wells. She was fortunate enough to have an 11-year-old owner who refused to give up hope and on one of his walks over the land where she was last seen he suddenly heard her bark coming from deep underground. Judy was dug out, emaciated but full of licks, and lived to tell the tale.

The second dog, Sam, got himself trapped inside a Gwent quarry for more than two weeks. He was finally reached by cavers but only after 100 tons of rock had been removed to create a 40 ft tunnel in an operation costing well over £1,000.

Then there was a Jack called Jane (if you follow), found by a poultry worker who'd sent his ferret down a hole to catch a rat. The ferret came back with a nasty bite on the nose that was clearly no rat bite – faint barks coming from below testified to that.

It took an hour to dig Jane out, putting an end to her 27 days without food or water in her deep, dark prison.

THE DOG HAD BEEN MISSING FOR 36 DAYS BUT HER YOUNG OWNER CONTINUED SEARCHING FOR HER.

Below: *Really, it's the only way to travel. This mutt in Redondo Beach, California, helps brighten the day for drivers stuck in jams. No other two species are as close as humankind and dogs.*

Above: *The memorial to Barry the St Bernard in Asnieres Cemetery, Paris. His skill and courage saved the lives of 40 people.*

In 1989 truck driver Ray Ashworth actually consulted a medium to discover the fate of his missing terrier Nipper. The little dog had been a passenger in Ray's parked car when it was snatched by joy riders. The car was found but Nipper was nowhere to be seen.

The psychic assured Ray he'd be reunited with his pet within 12 hours. It was a remarkable prediction ... for within three hours a 10-year-old girl rang him to say she'd picked up Nipper in a local park.

HAIRY HEROES

The cases of humans rescuing dogs and dogs rescuing humans seem to occur with roughly equal frequency. But perhaps the most famous and successful on the canine side are St Bernards, who over the years have been credited with saving the lives of more than 2,500 climbers and walkers stranded in the Alps.

They are particularly good at tracking and can scent out a live human being even if he or she is buried beneath 10 ft of snow. Their other mysterious talents include early warning of an avalanche, and of a blizzard approaching.

Among this much loved breed a dog called Barry, of the Hospice du Grand St Bernard in Switzerland, stands out as the most celebrated of all. In his career on the slopes he saved more than 40 lives, including that of a little boy stranded unconscious on an icy precipice after his mother was submerged by an avalanche.

Barry licked the youngster back to life, then persuaded him to climb up on his back for the treacherous journey back to the hospice.

When Barry at last became too old to perform his duties, the gallant hound was pensioned off to a good home in Berne, where he lived out his days in comfort until his death in 1814. His body was later stuffed and mounted and displayed in the Swiss Natural History Museum.

In Wales too, St Bernards have a reputation unmatched by any other breed. During one particularly cold winter, in 1981, a sheep farmer in the South Wales mountains discovered scores of his new-born lambs had been buried in deep snow. A dog called Bruno was brought in and promptly sniffed out 83 of them where the farm's Welsh collies had failed.

Yet there is an exception to every rule and in the case of the St Bernards the exception is a dog called George.

Where his breed made its name through efficiency, reliability and common sense, George excelled in being scatterbrained, stupid and generally clueless when out on a mission. His mountain rescue bosses finally lost patience when he was brought in to help track down two missing climbers and got himself detached from the main party.

Two hours later he still hadn't turned up and the rescuers had to locate the mountaineers on their own. They returned to base to find there was still no sign of the dog and a new search was mounted ... this time for George. It took them three hours to trace him and afterwards the rescuers were insistent: George would have to go. He'd got himself lost eight times in two years and in their neck of the woods they didn't need that kind of practice.

In Britain dogs served with great distinction during the last war and in 1943 Mrs Maria Dickin, founder of the People's Dispensary for Sick Animals, decided they should have their equivalent of the Victoria Cross, the nation's most prized medal.

First to be awarded the Dickin Medal was a cross-bred Labrador called Bob. His citation covered his immense skill and judgement in preventing an entire patrol of the Queen's Own Royal West Kent Regiment from being wiped out during a night operation in North Africa in January 1943.

Bob was leading the men near Green Hill but suddenly froze in his tracks, warning that the enemy was close by. The unit waited, but could hear nothing, and the commanding officer decided to move on. Bob refused to obey the order (an action that was technically a court martial offence) and the men again waited.

Then enemy movement was sighted and the patrol retreated safely without any casualties. Had they carried on they would have walked straight into enemy fire.

Strangely, Bob never returned to take the plaudits in Britain. In 1946 he was heading home through Milan airport but suddenly slipped his collar and went AWOL. He was never seen again, despite the best efforts of the War Office, who posted his description throughout Italy. In the end Bob's medal was collected by his owner, CQMS Cleggatt.

Of all the Dickin medallists none was better known than Judy, a pointer bitch born in Shanghai, who remains the only dog ever to be registered as an official prisoner of war.

Judy had served aboard a few Royal Navy gunboats in the Far East before being posted to HMS *Grasshopper* in 1942 as official mascot.

She saw action throughout the Malaya and Singapore campaigns and after the fall of Singapore found herself heading towards Java to await a supply ship rendezvous. However *Grasshopper* was bombed by the Japanese and forced to run aground, still blazing, on an uninhabited island. There she blew up, leaving the entire crew stranded.

From here on Judy's story reads like a script from some unlikely Hollywood war movie. She started by saving the lives of the sailors by discovering a fresh-water spring several miles up the seashore.

A few days later the castaways succeeded in commandeering a Chinese junk and a party set sail for Sumatra with the intention of organizing the rescue of their shipmates. Judy, of course, was on board.

But soon after landing they were caught by the Japanese and interned at a makeshift PoW camp at Medan. It was there that Judy was introduced to one Leading Aircraftsman Frank Williams, who shared his paltry rice rations with her. They quickly became the firmest of friends and Judy repaid the kindness she was shown

Above: *Judy, the only official dog prisoner of war. Her war against the Japanese reads like a Hollywood script.*

THE LABRADOR FROZE IN HIS TRACKS AND REFUSED TO BUDGE.

THE SADISTIC COMMANDANT ORDERED THE PRISONERS TO KILL AND EAT THEIR PET.

Right: Sheila, the border collie from England's wild Northumbrian hills, remains the only civilian dog to hold the Dickin Medal. She fought her way through a blinding snow storm to rescue the US crew of a crashed Flying Fortress plane.

many times, alerting Allied prisoners to poisonous animals such as snakes and scorpions ... as well as any Japanese guards that just happened to be snooping about.

Perhaps it was because she boosted morale so much that she infuriated the camp commandant. He tried to have her destroyed but with a mixture of superb diplomacy and bare-faced cheek LAC Williams contrived to get her registered as an official PoW.

Not to be outdone, the commandant ordered that Judy should stay at his camp after receiving orders that the rest of her comrades were to be shipped from Sumatra to Singapore. But again his wishes were defied and the plucky little pointer was smuggled aboard the prisoners' ship in a rice sack.

The following day the ship was torpedoed by the Allies and Judy was separated from her new master. But a miraculous twist of fate ensured that within three days they were back together at another prison camp.

After a tumultuous week LAC Williams and Judy could have been forgiven for trying to take a breather and simply gather their senses.

It was not to be. Their new commandant turned out to be the self-same thug they'd encountered at Medan. And, sure enough, one of his first orders was that Judy should be killed and eaten by the British prisoners by way of some unspecified punishment.

More than likely, this command was thought up as a twisted brand of revenge for Japan's imminent humiliation at the hands of the Americans. Fortunately it was never carried out. Judy was taken into hiding and the Japanese guards were too petrified of what would happen to them come the liberation of PoWs even to mount a search.

After the war Judy was brought back to England to receive her Dickin Medal. Her master got the White Cross of St Giles, the highest honour bestowed by the PDSA, in recognition of his courage in standing by Judy in some of her darkest hours.

He later revealed one touching story of her time as a PoW. She found an elephant's shin bone, still meaty, and decided Christmas and her birthday must have come along together. According to one

witness it was bigger than her and weighed far too much for her to carry properly. Yet in the best hound dog tradition she did manage to bury it ... even though it took her two laborious hours.

Only one civilian dog ever won the Dickin Medal – a young collie called Sheila owned by Northumberland shepherd John Dagg. She ventured out with him in a blinding snowstorm to track down and rescue the four-man crew of an American Flying Fortress which crashed in December 1944.

But in fact civilian disasters have provided ample opportunities down the centuries for humble hounds to shine out suddenly as heroes.

In one case, in 1919, the coaster *Ethie* was cruising off the coast of Nova Scotia when she ran into rocks in heavy seas. The mountainous waves washed all the lifeboats overboard and prevented rescuers from getting anywhere close. One man who fancied himself a powerful swimmer had already died in a futile attempt to swim for the shore.

Then Tang, a Newfoundland dog who bellyflopped straight into the treacherous seas, stepped forward and boldly struck out for the shore carrying a light line

Joyful hands pulled him to safety, a hawser was fixed to the line and minutes later the ship's hands were pulling it back and preparing a breeches buoy to take all 92 passengers and crew to safety. Even a baby was rescued, winched ashore in a mailbag.

Tang later received a medal for meritorious service from Lloyd's Insurance House of London, which he displayed proudly on his collar until the end of his days.

More than 100 years earlier a Newfoundland's swimming ability may actually have changed the course of history. In 1815 Napoleon was being smuggled out of exile on Elba to return to his beloved France. But he slipped on a rock as he prepared to board.

Panic set in (he was a hopeless swimmer) and as he splashed about helplessly his aides dashed hither and thither trying to spot him.

Eventually he was saved by a giant Newfoundland which plunged into the waters, grabbed the emperor by his shirt collar and towed him to waiting boatmen. Without that dog's actions there may well have been no return for Napoleon … and no battle of Waterloo.

The undisputed Mark Spitz of the canine kingdom though must surely be the appropriately named Neptune, a Newfoundland which was one among hundreds then carried by vessels as ever-ready life-savers. Neptune's ship was being towed up the Mississippi en route to New Orleans when it lurched violently, toppling the dog ignominiously into the river.

The captain was distraught to see his faithful hound left in the river but had no way to stop his ship without the help and co-operation of the skipper up front. He tearfully watched Neptune attempting to keep up with the two boats but eventually he began to fall back and soon disappeared from sight altogether. The captain comforted himself with the knowledge that Neptune would surely swim ashore and be picked up by some other salty types in need of his services.

He was wrong. Far from swimming ashore, Neptune kept on course along the Mississippi. Three days later, to his old shipmates' total amazement, he waltzed onto deck as though nothing was amiss.

He'd tracked them an incredible 50 miles, swimming against the current to New Orleans, and then somehow climbed the supply ships berthed around his own.

Neptune's achievement lay as much in his sense of smell as in his strength. Dogs are thought to have an olfactory system more than a million times more sensitive than humans – hence the achievements of St Bernards in the snow.

ROVING ROVERS

This is one explanation for some of the extraordinary distances a pet will travel to find an owner who has gone missing. But it is not always enough. Some scientists

Below: *Doug Sampson and his amazing German shepherd bitch Nick. She crossed snowbound mountains and deserts to get back to him.*

THE COLLIE WAS
DETERMINED TO HAVE
A DAY OUT IN LONDON –
AND HE PREFERRED TO
TRAVEL BY COACH.

believe animals may use some sort of navigation system based on the stars, though how they do it is a total mystery.

In 1923 a legendary collie called Bobbie was lost by his master during a holiday in Walcott, Indiana. Six months later Bobbie showed up at the family house in Silverton, Oregon, after travelling a distance of around 2,000 miles. When publicity on his journey leaked out many householders along the route stepped forward to say that they had seen Bobbie and offered him food and water. It was soon obvious that he had travelled through Illinois, Iowa, Nebraska and Colorado before negotiating the Rockies in the middle of winter and reaching home via Wyoming and Idaho.

Since then records show at least two German shepherd dogs have drawn on equally amazing homing instincts. The first, a bitch called Nick, was stolen while she and her master Doug Simpson were on a camping holiday in southern Arizona. After two weeks of looking for her a distraught Doug had to go home to Pennsylvania. By now heavy snow was blocking the mountain passes yet Nick had already disengaged herself from her captor and was homeward bound.

She eventually made it, successfully navigating both the Arizona Desert and the Grand Canyon, and turned up four months later at her master's car parked at his parents' house in Selah, Washington.

She'd sustained nasty wounds, and a poor diet had left her almost unrecognizable, but Nick later made a full recovery.

The second German shepherd to hit the headlines in a similar way managed a slight variation on the theme. Jessie decided she didn't want to move from her home in Rhode Island to Colorado. Hardly had her owner, Dexter Gardiner, finished arranging his furniture than Jessie pelted off and never looked back. She had apparently been pining for the rest of Dexter's family and the friendly dog next door.

The dog-homing phenomenon is also well documented in Australia. A little fox terrier called Whisky managed a 1,700-mile trek from Hayes Creek, south of Darwin, to Mambury Creek 150 miles north of Adelaide. And a labrador cross called Jimpa turned up at his old home in Pimpinio, Victoria, after a 2,000-mile hike across the nation's inhospitable central plains. It took him well over a year and how he ever survived remains a mystery.

Among the most sensible of all rovers was a British cross-bred collie called Spot who seemed to have an ambition to see the bright lights of London. In March 1983 he hopped on a National Express coach at Cardiff, refusing the driver's insistent

Right: *Yorkshire terrier Thumbelina was officially declared the world's smallest adult dog in 1993. What she lacks in size, she makes up for in beauty.*

requests to leave, and curled up on a front seat to sleep out the journey.

On arrival at London's Victoria coach station he cleaned himself up and jumped off for a look round. That was the last the driver thought he'd see of Spot … until the canny animal turned up a few hours later, just as the coach was about to begin the return leg of its 150-mile trip. At Cardiff Spot was taken in by the RSPCA and later claimed by his speechless owners.

There is little doubt, though, of the most travelled dog, not counting of course the 40 or so animals zoomed into outer space aboard the first experimental rockets. The terrestrial accolade has to go to a scruffy mongrel called Owney, who was said to have travelled well over 200,000 miles, both on land and sea, in his much vaunted career.

The Chinese have a saying that every great journey must begin with a small step and so it was for Owney when he padded in to a post office in Albany, New York, in 1888.

He was quickly adopted by the employees, who indulged his favourite pastime of riding on top of mailbags as they were ferried to the local railway depot. One day Owney decided it was time he stretched himself a little more, so he boarded a mail train for New York City. That was just the start.

In the years that followed Owney was a regular sight on trains as they criss-crossed the country. His old friends at Albany couldn't help worrying about him, though, so they attached a tag to his collar asking clerks along the route to fix metallic baggage labels to his collar so that a full record could be kept of his travels.

Owney picked up so many tags that a special jacket was made for him to display them on. He received it from the Postmaster General during a visit to Washington and became so proud of his flashy coat that anyone who touched a tag got an ominous growl for his trouble.

As the years slipped by Owney notched up Canada and Mexico, but the unique highlight of his life was a round-the-world trip set up for him by postal workers at Tacoma, Washington.

From that city Owney called at Yohohama, Shanghai, Woosung, Foochow, Hong Kong, Singapore, Suez, Algiers and the Azores before making it back to New

York and the commuter train back to Tacoma.

Throughout this time he was welcomed everywhere he went. Railmen regarded him as a lucky omen for no train that carried him ever encountered a mishap.

But as with all travelling there is an element of danger and Owney's own luck ran out on 11 June 1897.

By then he was well into old age and able to eat only the softest of foods and water, but he still managed the occasional railcar ride and on that day had taken the

Above: *You've seen them scuba-diving and motorbiking. Now meet the original jet-skiing Alsatian!*

Above: *Billy the champion ratter. In 1825 he caused a sensation in the rat-pits of London, killing 4,000 vermin in 17 hours. In his heyday he was supposed to have despatched one rat every 3.24 seconds.*

train to Toledo. No one ever gave a clear account of exactly what happened but it appears Owney suddenly became 'ill-tempered' while being introduced to a local journalist. Perhaps the man touched one of his 1,017 tags and tokens. Or perhaps, like many stars before and since, Owney just didn't like the press.

Either way the much loved mongrel was shot and killed with a single bullet. His body was later stuffed and exhibited in Washington DC's Smithsonian Institute.

Britain's answer to Owney was a fox-terrier called Jack. And what he lacked in distance travelled, he made up for in social climbing.

Such was his fame that in 1883 he was presented to the then prince and princess of Wales, one of only a handful of mutts to be honoured by an official visit from royalty.

Jack's train-hopping life was centred on the Sussex town of Lewes in southern England. From here he would explore the whole south-eastern rail network, though he was particularly partial to the now defunct Brighton and Horsham line.

In 1881 the *Illustrated Sporting and Dramatic News* reported a typical day in Jack's life: 'He arrived from Brighton by train, reaching Steyning at 10.50 where he got out for a minute but then went on by the same train to Henfield. Here he popped in to a public house not far from the station where a biscuit was given to him and after a little walk he took a later train to West Grinstead where he spent the afternoon, returning to Brighton in time for the last train to Lewes.'

Jack sported a silver-plated collar inscribed 'I am Jack, the London Brighton and South Coast Railway Dog. Please give me a drink and I will then go home to Lewes.' He appears to have taken his semi-official status very seriously. On the day of the funeral of the Eastbourne station inspector Jack turned up by train and followed the hearse to the cemetery. He even walked to the graveside to pay his last respects.

The little dog's exploits brought him

close to death himself. On one occasion he wandered on to the line at Norwood Junction, south London, and was hit by a train which crushed one of his front legs. Railmen who saw the accident rushed him onto a fast train to Lewes where two vets were forced to amputate his useless leg. But it didn't stop his travelling and he got about on three legs just as well as on four.

Jack eventually retired at the same time as the Lewes stationmaster and joined him to live at Mayfield in Sussex. But the two of them would still make the occasional journey – first class of course.

Yet occasionally Jack would creep back to his favourite spot: nothing, it seemed, could match the comfort of the guard's van.

SHAGGY DOG STORIES

His fame among the dogs of 19th-century England was probably matched only by an animal of doubtful parentage who became the nation's champion ratter.

Billy, who weighed in at 26 lb, would compete in rat-killing matches and apparently won his first ten contests with such ease it became almost boring for the bloodthirsty spectators.

In 1825 he was reported to have despatched 4,000 rats in just 17 hours, an incredible achievement considering he was blind in one eye. Other claims made for him include the killing of 100 rats in 1/2 minutes, although this particular exhibition was not covered by a later rule prohibiting dog handlers from touching either dog or rats.

Billy was even said to have notched up 000 rats in 54 minutes, though this was surely an exaggeration considering that he'd have had to kill an average of one every 3.24 seconds. In those days one kill every 5 seconds was considered champion form.

Even in his old age Billy could still draw a crowd to a rat pit. At 10 years old he outshone a younger rival by sending 0 rats to meet their maker in 8 minutes seconds. The younger dog took minutes to accomplish the same task.

Tales of dogs as killing machines are legion. In both Europe and the US much has been made of the ferocity of pit bull terriers, trained to savage each other.

Certainly one family from Devon, England, learned to their cost the savagery of a pit bull. It went berserk and wrecked their home after being stung by a wasp. The dog, Smudge, caused around £1,000 damage by tearing apart furniture, smashing windows and chewing through a door. One vet called to calm the dog said later: 'It looked like a hostage shootout, as if the SAS had been in there.'

Not all reputations stand up to the test, however. In 1990 a British Rottweiler called Rossita, on a diet because she was failing to impress show judges, tried to steal the family rabbit's carrot lunch.

The rabbit, aptly called Rambo, took exception and turned on the terrified hound, seeing her off with a lacerated nose, cuts and bruises ... and a severely damaged ego.

> **THE PIT BULL WENT BERSERK WHEN IT WAS STUNG BY A WASP.**

Below: *Police super-dog Trep. Cadets at a training school were once told to hide ten packets of marijuana for him to track down. Trep found 11.*

THE TRAIL WAS 8 YEARS OLD – BUT THE DOG SNIFFED OUT THE MURDERER WITH EASE.

Talking of doggie egos, a 15-year-old mongrel called Ari actually sued the American airline USAir for allegedly causing him to circle pointlessly around a baggage claim carousel while his owner had vanished into thin air.

Ari's owner was a lawyer, who immediately slapped in a $60,000 compensation demand for the temporary loss of his best friend. The writ was filed in the dog's name but kicked out on the orders of a judge who ruled that dogs were not American citizens.

Other legal firsts include the case of a poodle who sought registration, via her owner, for Abbey National plc shares. The bank turned the mutt down on the grounds she was only a trustee account holder.

Then there was the Surrey sheep farmer who bought a pedigree Welsh collie only to find it had been taught in Welsh and didn't understand his commands. He tried to persuade his local trading standards department to sue ... but the case never got off the ground.

Some dogs, like humans, just seem to be born lucky. One Italian Alsatian, Gunther, was actually left £65 million by his owner and ended up getting begging letters from cash-strapped soccer clubs.

But others have to work for a living and what could be more satisfying than a job with the police?

Duke, the first guard dog to work for the Metropolitan Police in London, seemed set for a distinguished career – until he found himself fingered. For weeks there had been a series of thefts from handbags in the typing pool at Brixton nick and an insider was suspected. Then one typist noticed Duke nosing about in her bag and his dirty deeds were exposed.

Many mutts, though, do serve with flying colours. Some breeds with a particularly sensitive sense of smell are much sought after as crimefighters. For them, the trail of a crook can last weeks or even years.

A German shepherd delightfully named Harass II offers perfect proof of this. On 19 January 1974 the body of an unknown woman was found in scrubland close to the Kennedy Space Center near Titusville, Florida. For years dozens of leads were followed without success but on 22 July 1982 fresh information emerged and a suspect was pulled in.

Murder squad detectives tried to break him down without success. Believing they'd got their man, but unsure how to proceed, they called in Harass as a last-shot attempt to see if he could turn anything up. He was given some clothing owned by the suspect to sniff and about half a mile from where the woman's body was found, Harrass picked up a trail. He led police to a different spot and the officers concluded this must have been where the murder actually took place.

They returned to the suspect armed with this new information. Convinced they must have a strong case against him he admitted his crime and made a full confession.

The time between murder and tracking was an incredible eight years, six months and three days.

Among many other famous police dogs special credit must go to a drug sniffing specialist called Trep.

On his first assignment in Florida he was being taken to sniff around a boat at Fort Lauderdale when he suddenly made a break for it and headed for a racing sloop that had already been painstakingly hand searched four times by agents. Trep boarded the vessel and located $2. million worth of hashish (1973 prices) hidden in a false wall.

This animal later went on to break new legal ground when a judge issued him with a search warrant to check out house where drugs had earlier been identified. The police found a massive hoard of marijuana inside.

But Trep's best-known – and best loved coup – came when he visited police academy to show off his skills. His handler gave cadets marijuana to hide anywhere they wished on the premises. Ten packets were handed out. Trep found eleven.